Order this book online at www.trafford.com/08-0570
or email orders@trafford.com

Most Trafford titles are also available at major online book retailers.

Book layout design: Sheltom (Pvt.) Ltd.
Cover Design: Sheltom (Pvt.) Ltd.
Shelley Craven
advertising sheltom UK
sheltom92@aol.com
mobile: +44 780 672 6965
All photographs by Kenneth P. Williams

© Copyright 2008 Kenneth P. Williams.
All rights reserved. No part of this publication may be reproduced, stored in a retrieval system, or transmitted, in any form or by any means, electronic, mechanical, photocopying, recording, or otherwise, without the written prior permission of the author.

Note for Librarians: A cataloguing record for this book is available from Library and Archives Canada at www.collectionscanada.ca/amicus/index-e.html

ISBN: 978-1-4251-7756-0

www.trafford.com

North America & international
toll-free: 1 888 232 4444 (USA & Canada)
phone: 250 383 6864 ♦ fax: 250 383 6804
email: info@trafford.com

The United Kingdom & Europe
phone: +44 (0)1865 487 395 ♦ local rate: 0845 230 9601
facsimile: +44 (0)1865 481 507 ♦ email: info.uk@trafford.com

10 9 8 7 6 5 4 3 2 1

Dedicated to my mother, Alice Williams, who would have said, I am sure, "Ooooh Kenneth."

" To laugh often and much; to win the respect of intelligent people and the affection of children; to earn the appreciation of honest critics and endure the betrayal of false friends; to appreciate beauty, to find the best in others; to leave the world a little better, whether by a healthy child, a garden patch or a redeeemed social condition; to know even one life has breathed easier because you have lived. This is the meaning of success."

Ralph Waldo Emerson.

FRONT COVER PICTURE:
Jules Verne's grave in Cimetiere de La Madeleine, Amiens, France.

BACK COVER PICTURE:
Robert Thibier's grave in Le Cimetiere Montparnasse, Paris, France.

INTRODUCTION

My first recollection of visiting a cemetery was in about 1975. I was on holiday in North Wales and decided to see if I could locate my Great Grandfather's grave which was in a cemetery near Caernarfon. My father had described roughly where I should find it and so off I went.

The weather was inclement and the long grass made the bottoms of my jeans soaking wet. There were many dark and grim looking headstones skilfully created from slate from local mines and it didn't look as if anyone cared about these people any more. After all they were once somebody's family, but their names had been forgotten in the mists of time.

You may think that this may not be the most exciting way to spend your time by visiting cemeteries and churchyards, but I am sure that after thumbing through this publication you may develop a different view on the subject.

In this book I have tried to create an assemblage of graves of a varied nature. You will find the rich and famous mixed with the ordinary people but the common denominator is that they all have a story to tell or an event to describe.

Something that they did or that happened to them in the near or distant past. It is important that everyone has their fifteen minutes of fame although I would accept that some may have had more than their fair share already.

On my travels I have come across cemeteries in quite differing environments. The cemetery in Iceland was covered in snow and ice, not surprisingly. In Singapore and Thailand it was very hot and humid. The Caribbean was hot and dry. Elsewhere the climate could have been
wet, warm or cold, different everywhere that I travelled.

You will find the graves in this book arranged in no particular order. They are presented to you as they are and not categorised either in alphabetical of regional order. This is because you will find that graves are not generally arranged in any particular order within a cemetery or a churchyard, except perhaps chronologically in the order that they passed away. Take them as you find them and indulge yourself in their past lives.

My thanks are extended to all those who have aided the production of this book especially Jeannette, my dear wife, who gave herself the title of 'research assistant' for all the help that she gave to me on those rainy days when we trudged

up and down rows of headstones, day after day, looking for interesting graves. She also spent hours proof-reading this document, so I thank you Jeannette.

You could be forgiven for thinking that I prefer the company of the departed to the company of the here present, but I can assure you that this is not the case.

My apologies if I have miss quoted any of the text from the headstone entries in this publication, but as you may be aware, sometimes it is very difficult to read some of the letters or words on the headstones due to their age or the natural growth of vegetation that is attached to them. I also apologise for not typing any correct accents such as in Iceland and France, but my keyboard did not have the necessary keys.

I truly believe that for everybody who has lived and died in this world whether they were known throughout the world or known only to their mother and father that if we say their name once more then they have 'lived' again and that they have not been forgotten.

JULES VERNE

Grave Text:
'Jules Verne. Ne a Nantes Le 8 Fevrier 1828 Decede a Amiens Le 24 Mars 1905.' Rough Translation: Born in Nantes 8th February 1828 Died in Amiens 24th March 1905.

Situated: Cimetiere de La Madeleine, Amiens, France.

Authors Comment: Jules Verne was a French Writer; his novels include "Journey To The Center Of The Earth", "Twenty Thousand Leagues Under The Sea" & "Around The World In Eighty Days". His writings were done prior to any regular air, space or underwater travel and as such were visionary. He was called by some, the 'Father of Science Fiction'. His grave is most striking with (presumably) Verne breaking from his tomb and reaching for the stars. The laurel branches represent a special achievement, distinction and success.

LENA STOKES

Grave Text:
'In Loving Memory of Lena Stokes 10.7.1898 : 13.1.1995. GORN BUT NOT FORGOTTEN.'

Situated: St George's Anglican Cathedral, Kingstown, St Vincent, Caribbean.

Authors Comment: There are two angels on the headstone which represent the messengers between God and man. 'Gorn But Not Forgotten' is a nice sentiment, well said!

FRANK CHRISTOPHER GRAHAM

Grave Text:
'In Loving Memory of Frank Christopher Graham.
Nov. 1926 – Oct. 2002
WINDOW DECORATOR
DESIGNER PAREXCELLENT
Rest In Peace.'

Situated:
St Mary's Church, Barbados, Caribbean.

Authors Comment:
Small white marble headstone.
This gentleman was obviously good at his profession, and well respected for it.

HARRIET HUSBANDS

Grave Text:
'This stone is here placed to mark where the remains of Harriet Husbands lie, who died on the 10 of July 1844, aged 63 years & also to show where her son Sinclair Mackenzie & his family are to be buried should they die in Barbados.
The remains of James Pairman Esqr., Mrs Mackenzie's Father are also deposited here. He was Post Master of this Island 33 years & died on the 6th. Of Decr. 1845, aged 60 years.'

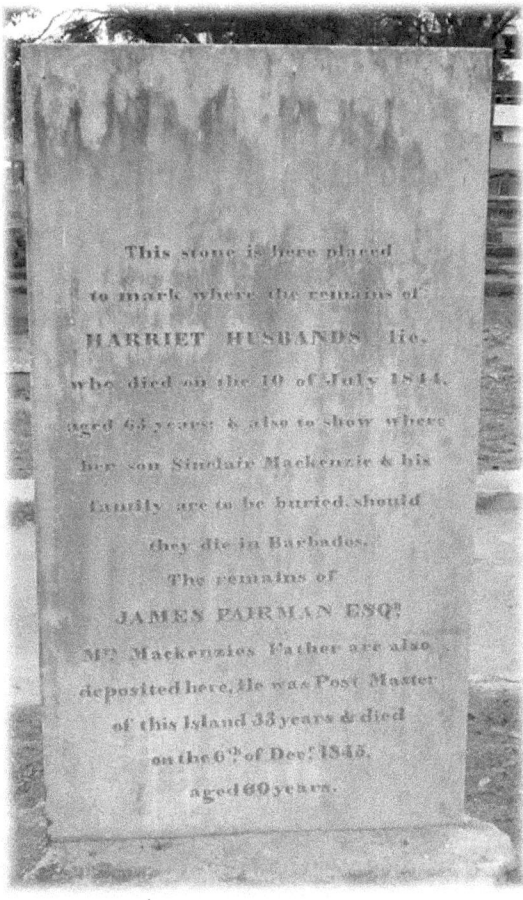

Situated:
St Mary's Church, Barbados, Caribbean.

Authors Comment:
Large erect ectangular stone or concrete headstone.
It is unusual to state on a gravestone the names of people who can be buried in the future but with conditions applied. A person's occupation and length of service provided helps to present a greater picture of them.

James Pairman, Harriet's father, was a long standing respected person in the local society, being a Post Master.

A SOLDIER OF THE GREAT WAR

Grave Text:
'A Soldier of the Great War, 20th Bn London Regiment. Known unto God.'

Situated:
Warlencourt British Cemetery (Commonwealth War Graves), Warlencourt, Pas-de-Calais, France.

Authors Comment: The badge of the 20th Battalion The London Regiment, with its motto "Invicta", which means "Unconquered", is engraved on the top of this headstone.

One of many hundreds of thousands of graves from the 1st World War where a soldier is buried but their name is not known. In this case they were able to state from which Regiment he served, possibly from his uniform, a button or a badge. The comment 'Known unto God' on this is very poignant.

THOMAS WORTH AND JOHN BUCKLAND

Grave Text:
'To the Memory of Lieutenants Thomas Worth and John Buckland of the Royal Marine Artillery who were Killed by the same Shot on the 23rd November 1810 while directing the Howitzer Boats in an attack on the Enemy's Flotilla in Cadiz Bay. Their Brother Officers on the same station have caused this Stone to be erected as a tribute of respect to two who were the brightest ornaments of their Corps.'

Situated:
Trafalgar Cemetery, Gibraltar.

Authors Comment:
A white marble plaque within a stone built surround. An unusual joint grave with both Officers meeting their end by the same shot. Contains history in the text and also shows the amount of respect that the two gentlemen had from their fellow Officers. The great loss is also to the Navy it appears, as they were 'the brightest ornaments of their Corps'.

PIERCE LLOYD

Grave Text:
'Hereunder lyeth...Body of Pierce Lloyd, Drover who dyed August 8 Anno Dom 1712 Aged 40 leaving 4 children by his wife & ....R....Mary who in sorrow dedicates this to his memory.'

Situated:
Saint Deiniol Church, Llanddeiniolen, Arfon, Gwynedd, North Wales.

Authors Comment:
A very old grave with a scull & crossbones engraved upon. The skull and crossbones represent death. Quite an unusual engraving on a gravestone in a Church graveyard but one which was used in the period of this monument.

RICHARD HUGHES

Grave Text:
'Here lyeth the body of Richard Hughes gentle m'n who was intered the 4 day of …..ember anno domini 1702 aged …. Also Dorothy bur'd his wife. Also Mary Lloyd   Richard Evans bur' '.

Situated:
The Church of Saint Mary, Caerhun, Conwy Valley, North Wales.

Authors Comment:
The Church is sited on the remains of the Roman fort of Canovium. Parts of the Church date back as far as the 13th century. This Gravestone is to be found as part of the external roof structure. It is actually on the north west gable, a most unusual but practical use I feel. It is still quite legible although it is upside down.

SERGEANT A. H. L. RICHARDSON V.C.

Grave Text:
'Within this cemetery lies Sergeant A.H.L.Richardson V.C. of Lord Strathcona's Horse (Royal Canadians) 1872 - 1932 Awarded the Victoria Cross 5th July 1900 at Wolwespruit, South Africa. The first man to win the V.C. while serving with a Canadian unit under British command.'

Situated:
St James Cemetery, Liverpool Anglican Cathedral, Liverpool, England.

Authors Comment:
The engraving of a large Victoria Cross adorns the headstone and the citation for this V.C. reads:
"On the 5th July 1900, at Wolve Spruit, about 15 miles north of Standerton, a party of Lord Strathcona's Corps, only thirty eight in number, came into contact, and was engaged at close quarters, with a force of eighty of the enemy. When the order to retire had been given, Sergeant Richardson rode back under a very heavy cross-fire and picked up a trooper whose horse had been shot and who was wounded in two places and rode with him out of fire. At the time when this act of gallantry was performed, Sergeant Richardson was within 300 yards of the enemy and was himself riding a wounded horse."
Although Richardson's V.C. was conferred by Queen Victoria, it was actually presented by King Edward VII on 12th March 1901, as Queen Victoria sadly died on 22nd January 1901 at Osborne House on the Isle of White.

MARY ALLEN

Grave Text:
'In Loving Memory of Mary Allen aged 46 years, who with her son Ernest was drowned at sea December 3rd 1909 through the disaster to the "SS Ellan Vannin."
Also of Ernest Allen aged 15 years whose body was recovered and was here interred December 20th 1909.'

Situated:
St James Cemetery, Liverpool Anglican Cathedral, Liverpool, England.

Authors Comment:
The Ellan Vannin (the Manx name for the Isle of Man) was an iron paddle steamer built in 1860 in Glasgow. She sank in a storm in Liverpool Bay with the loss of all life, thirty six souls, on 3rd December 1909 on her way from Ramsey, Isle of Man, to Liverpool. Soon after the sinking the Mersey Docks and Harbour Board blew up the wreck as it was causing a hazard to other shipping in the channel.
A song by The Spinners commemorates the disaster.
The Spinners were a 1960's folk group from Liverpool who produced over forty albums, retiring in 1989 having completed 30 years together.

LIVERPOOL ORPHAN BOYS' ASYLUM

Grave Text:
'Robert H Winter aged 12 years died 17 May 1837. Thomas Jackson aged 12 years died 23 July 1860. John Twist aged 12 years died 3 Decr. 1861. Owen Hughes aged 9 years died 18 June 1863. John Price aged 9 years died 24 June 1863. John Ross aged 14 years died 28 Novr. 1863.

Edward Atkinson aged 10 years died 11 Feby. 1864. William Kissock aged 9 years died 9 March 1865. John Smith aged 8 years died 5 Novr. 1866. Willm. Hy Bird aged 13 years died 11 Novr.1866. Robert Main aged 13 years died 31 July 1867. Gideon Hudson aged 9 years died 30 May 1878. Wm. Atherton aged 9 years died 2 Jany. 1875. John J. Williams aged 14 years died 24 Feby. 1886. Robt. Woodhall aged 11 years died 11 April 1886. Walter Holt aged 15 years died 27 Feby. 1889. John Robt. Norris aged 32 years died 29 Decr. 1890. Richd. Hamblett aged 12 years died 21 Octr. 1894.'

Situated:
St James Cemetery, Liverpool Anglican Cathedral, Liverpool, England.

Authors Comment:
One of many orphanages in Liverpool, The Liverpool Orphan Boys' Asylum was situated in Myrtle Street, Liverpool, England. In an 1895 list of Orphanages in Liverpool the Matron then was listed as Miss F.A. Finch.

JOHN FOSTER ESQ.

Grave Text:
Sacred to the memory of John Foster Esq: of this grave. Architect.
Who died on the 21st day of August 1846 aged 59 years.
Also Mary Anne Foster the daughter of Robert Foster and niece of the above John Foster. Died 10th September 1850 aged 38 years.
Also Marianne, wife of the above John Foster: Died 14th October 1862 aged 75 years.'

Situated:
St James Cemetery, Liverpool Anglican Cathedral, Liverpool, England.

Authors Comment:
John Foster Jnr. was an English Architect. He succeeded his father as Senior Surveyor to the Corporation of Liverpool in 1824. His own designs include The Oratory and the dramatic St James Cemetery, both in the grounds of Liverpool Anglican Cathedral. He is also responsible for St. Andrew's Church in Rodney Street, Liverpool, the second Royal Infirmary and public baths (both now demolished) and the domed Custom House in Liverpool, which suffered superficial damage during WWII.

HENRY T WILDE

Grave Text:
'In Loving Memory of Mary Catherine (Polly) the dearly beloved wife of Lieut. Henry T Wilde R.N.R. who departed this life 24th Decr 1910 aged 38 years. Also the twin sons of the above Archie and Richard who died in infancy Decr 1910. A loving mother and a faithful friend. Also the above Captn Henry T Wilde R.N.R. Acting Chief Officer who met his death in the "S.S. Titanic" disaster 15th April 1912 aged 38 years.

One of Britain's heroes.'

Situated:
Kirkdale Cemetery, Longmoor Lane, Aintree, Liverpool, England.

Authors Comment:
A tall memorial in pink granite with an urn with crepe on the top which signifies 'mourning'. Henry Wilde was born in Walton, Liverpool, England. His apprenticeship began in 1889 onboard the vessel "Greystoke Castle", and in 1897 he joined the White Star Line.
Wilde became Chief Officer of the "RMS Olympic" in 1911. He was assigned as Titanic's Chief Officer at the last minute in 1912.
Titanic sailed 10th April 1912 and Wilde reported for duty at 6am that day. At 11.40pm on 14th April, Titanic struck an iceberg and sank. The rest is history. It has been said, although it is impossible to prove, that Wilde was the officer who committed suicide, with his pistol, in the last minutes of the sinking.

ORMAND J. OLLIVIERRE

Grave Text:
'Warmest Memory of our Dear Beloved Ormond J Ollivierre who was Assassinated on April 30, 1980 at the age of 51 years'.

Situated:
St Georges Anglican Cathedral, Kingstown, St Vincent, Caribbean.

Authors Comment:
A stone or concrete headstone painted grey placed upon a bed of 'crazy paving' picked out in white.
It is quite striking to read that this gentleman died through being assassinated.

EDWIN SLACK (E. JONES)

Grave Text:
'Edwin Slack served as 9553 Private E. Jones Manchester Regiment 12th August 1918 aged 32.'

Situated:
Villers-Bretonneux Military Cemetery (Commonwealth War Graves), Somme, France.

Authors Comment:
The badge of the Manchester Regiment appears on the headstone with its motto "Concilio Et Labore", which means "Wisdom and Effort".

It appears that this soldier wanted to serve under an alias for reasons known only to himself. Slack being his true family name.

Villers-Bretonneux became famous in 1918, when the German advance on Amiens ended in the capture of the village by their tanks and infantry on 23 April. On the following day, the 4th and 5th Australian Divisions, with units of the 8th and 18th Divisions, recaptured the whole of the village and on 8 August 1918, the 2nd and 5th Australian Divisions advanced from its eastern outskirts in the Battle of Amiens. VILLERS-BRETONNEUX MILITARY CEMETERY was made after the Armistice when graves were brought in from other burial grounds in the area and from the battlefields.

CAPTAIN HUGH WILLIAMS

Grave Text:
'Diogel Yn Mreichiau Fy Ngwaredwr Gr Serc Hag GofA M Captain Hugh Williams (Caegwydryn) Anwyl Briod Jane Williams Yr Hwn A Hunodd Rhagfyr 24 1913 Yn 56 Ml Oed Hefyd Thomas Henry Mab Bychan Yr Uchod Yr Hwn A Fu Farw Tachwedd 3, 1884.
Hefyd Jane Annwyl Briod Yr Uchod A Fu Farw Medi 28, 1941 Yn 85 Ml Oed Hefyd ei mab.

William Griffith Gollwyd Yn "Ffrainc" Hydref 1916 Yn 19 Ml Oed "Gorphwys Maent Mewd Hedd" .' Translated roughly to English: Safe in the arms of my redeemer/saviour. In respectful remembrance of Captain Hugh Williams (Caegwydryn) Dear husband of Jane Williams who died 24th December 1913 aged 56. Also Thomas Henry little son of the above who died 3rd November 1884. Also Jane dear wife of the above who died 28th September 1941 aged 85. Also their son William Griffith Lost in France October 1916 aged 19. "They Rest In Peace" '.

Situated:
St Mary's Church Cemetery, Griffiths Crossing, Llanfair-Is-Gaer, Gwynedd, North Wales.

Authors Comment:
Nice grave with the carved anchor signifying a mariner ie. Captain Hugh Williams. The vines represent a firm Christian faith. On a life belt is 'Diogei yn Mreichiau fy Ngwaredwr'.
Hugh served on many ships including the "Alice Davies", which sank in Liverpool Bay in 1878, and the "S.S.England". He sailed to places far a field such as America & Australia. Whilst living in Wales he captained ships taking slate from the Dinorwic Quarry around the coast to other British Ports for roofing etc. William Griffiths Williams was killed at the Battle of the Somme in France on 1st October 1916. He joined up to the King's Liverpool Regiment in Kirkdale, Liverpool and was ultimately transferred to the 1/20th Battalion London Regiment. William was sent for embarkation to France in August 1916 and was killed two months later at Eaucourt l'Abbaye, near Warlencourt with 101 other soldiers from his regiment. His name is listed on the Thiepval Memorial, France, as his body was never recovered. Such a waste of human life.

CAPTAIN THOMAS S JONES

Grave Text:
'Capt Thomas S Jones, Sea View Terrace, Port Dinorwic. Fu Farw Hyd 16 1885 Yn 60 Ml Oed Ac Aw. Henry Ei Fab Yr Hwn A Foddodd Yn Afon Lerpwl Drwy Suddiad Y Llestr Alice Davies Tach 21 1878 Yn 17 Ml Oed. Hefyd Am Jane Jones. Gweddw Yr Uchod Yr Hon Farw Iona Wr 3 1900 Yn 76 Mloed. Gwyn fyd preswylwyr dy: yn wastad Y'Th Foliannant.'

Translated roughly to English: Captain Thomas S Jones, Sea View Terrace, Port Dinorwic. Who died October 16th 1885 aged 60 and Henry, son of the above who was drowned in the Liverpool river through the sinking of the vessel Alice Davies on 21st November 1878, aged 17. Also Jane Jones widow of the above who died 3rd January 1900 aged 76. Blessed are they that dwell in thy house, they will be still praising thee. Psalm 84.4'.

Situated:
St Mary's Church Cemetery, Griffiths Crossing, Llanfair-Is-Gaer, Gwynedd, North Wales.

Authors Comment:
The headstone is made from Welsh Slate which was probably quarried in the local Dinorwic Quarries. On the top it has a flower which represents fragility of life and with a severed stem it represents a shortened life. There is a double link to another grave which is described in this book, that of Captain Hugh Williams.
The first link is that Henry Jones actually drowned when the "Alice Davies", sank in Liverpool Bay on the 21st November 1878 on its way to Adelaide with a general cargo (Hugh was also on this ship). It was 'run down' and sank by the Steamship Cherbourg with the loss of five lives including Henry. The "Alice Davies", No: 58941, Code H.L.Q.T. was a Barque made of iron. She had a tonnage of 608 gross, and was built in Liverpool by R & J Evans. At the time of the sinking she was owned by D W Davies & Co of Brunswick Street, Liverpool. Henry's wages for the voyage would have been two pound per week, and from the ship's log three shillings were paid out in lieu of these wages after the sinking, presumably to the next of kin. The second link is that Captain Hugh Williams eventually married Henry's sister Jane Jones on the 28th August 1882. This grave is next but one to that of Captain Hugh Williams in the same cemetery.

JAMES BLANCHARD

Grave Text:
'In Memoriam.
James Blanchard died Augt 20. 1875 aged 19.
Drowned whilst bathing under Llanfair.
Jesu Mercy'.

Situated:
St Mary's Church Cemetery, Griffiths Crossing, Llanfair-Is-Gaer, Gwynedd, North Wales.

Authors Comment:
Made of Welsh Slate with a prominent cross on the top. The cross is an emblem of faith.
A simple inscription but still states the details of a tragic end to his young life.

WILLIAM LORT F.R.G.S.

Grave Text:
'In affectionate remembrance of William Lort F.R.C.S. late of Fron Goch Hall, Llanllugan, Montgomeryshire who died at Vaynol Old Hall May 23rd 1891 at the age of 69. A Great Traveller and Explorer and a Noted Judge of Animals.'

Situated:
St Mary's Church Cemetery, Griffiths Crossing, Llanfair-Is-Gaer, Gwynedd, North Wales.

Authors Comment:
Very attractive tomb made from pink granite.
The deceased appears to have been a well respected and well travelled gentleman who was a Fellow of the Royal Geographical Society. Mr Lort's speciality was in the field of animals.

SIR LLEWELYN TURNER

Grave Text:

'Sacred to and in loving memory of Sir Llewelyn Turner born at Parkia February 11 1823 and died there 18 September 1903 "What e'er was true he loved" Sacred to the memory of Dame Agnes Turner widow of the said Sir Llewelyn Turner of Parkia Carnarvon Died 13 March 1926 age 73 years.

And with the morn those angel faces smile which I have loved long since and lost a while'.

Situated:
St Mary's Church Cemetery, Griffiths Crossing, Llanfair-Is-Gaer, Gwynedd, North Wales.

Authors Comment:
This grave is marked with a grand headstone in the shape of a rock. On this is an anchor with a chain and a life belt and chain, with a wreath to top this off. The anchor is for hope and represents a seafaring profession and the wreath is for victory.

This is indeed a grave of some standing with low iron railings around and three ornamental shells in marble, although sadly it is now overgrown with weeds and brambles.

Sir Llewelyn Turner was a great benefactor of Caernarfon. He was Mayor from 1859 to 1870 and then Deputy Constable of Caernarfon Castle for some 30 years. He was instrumental in renovating the castle from a ruin to the magnificent fortress it is now and was a fitting venue for the investiture of Prince Charles in 1969.

GEORGE & KITTY SMITH

Grave Text:
'George & Kitty Smith 1720.'

Situated:
St. Aidens Church Graveyard, Billinge, Lancashire, England.

Authors Comment:
A most unusual and interesting tombstone this, as it is shaped like a coffin and has the carving of a skull surrounded by a serpent. There is something carved above the skull but is too weathered to read now.

It is extremely old and is dated 1720, which is just visible and nearly obscured by the snake carving.

Quite similar to another gravestone listed in this book, that of Pierce Lloyd, but with a skull and serpent instead of the skull and crossbones.

In this case the skull represents mortality and the serpent with its tail in its mouth represents everlasting life in heaven.

WILLIAM ALEXANDER

Grave Text:
'To the memory of William Alexander LLD Citizen Journalist Author. In the pages of "Johnny Gibb" is portrayed with rare fidelity and charm the character and ways of his "Ain Folk" in Aberdeenshire. Born 12th June 1826. Died 19th February 1894. His wife Anne Allan 1832 - 1922'.

Situated:
Aberdeen Nellfield Cemetery, Aberdeen, Scotland.

Authors Comment:
William Alexander was best known for his novel "Johnny Gibb of Gushetneuk" which was published in 1871. It was also serialised in the Aberdeen Free Press for which he became a journalist after loosing a leg in an accident when he was 20 years old. Prior to this he worked on a farm. He wrote five other novels but these were not as respected as his first novel.

The Head stone was erected by public subscription.

It is a prominent memorial with a bust presumably of William Alexander himself on top of a plinth. It is a mixture of stone including red, grey and black granite.

PETER MILNE

Grave Text:
'In this paupers grave lies Peter Milne a famous violinist and composer of Scottish music 1824 – 1908.
The Tarland Minstrel.
Erected by The Scottish Fiddle College and the Elphinstone Institute'.

Situated:
Aberdeen Nellfield Cemetery, Aberdeen, Scotland.

Authors Comment:
Peter Milne, which is pronounced "Mill", was a prolific fiddler who was born in Kincardine O'Neil (the oldest village in Deeside) and moved to Tarland in his youth. He was well travelled through his music. Married to Isabella they had seven children. Peter had been a music teacher and led orchestras at a number of theatres in Scotland. Queen Victoria presented him with a silver medal for his rendering of 'Auld Robin Gray' which he performed at Balmoral for her. He apparently became an opium addict after using the drug for his rheumatism and spent the last ten years of his life in hospital after becoming an invalid. It is said that he fell when someone removed a chair he was to sit on. He died in Aberdeen Poorhouse in 1908 (hence the paupers grave).
There is also a monument to Peter Milne in Tarland Square, which was erected in 1932.

ALEXANDER AITKEN WATT

Grave Text:

'Erected by John Watt stone cutter and pavement merchant Aberdeen in memory of his family. James Craighead died in infancy 1873. Jessie Scott born 30th July 1874 died 23rd March 1896. Edward William, born 22nd March 1885 died 23rd February 1898. Alexander Aitken, Volunteered in the Imperial Yeomanry during the S.A. War. Born 29th August 1881 and was killed in action at Aberdeen Cape Colony 6th March 1901. Mary Ann Craighead wife of John Watt, Born 22nd July 1852 died 26th April 1911. Also the said John Watt born 27th March

1850 died 5th October 1926. "Till the resurrection morn" '.
Situated:
Aberdeen Nellfield Cemetery, Aberdeen, Scotland.

Authors Comment:
John Watt being a stone cutter would I feel sure have been proud of this memorial in black granite. Alexander was in the Imperial Yeomanry which was a British volunteer cavalry and saw most of its action in the Second Boar War. It was made up of existing Yeomanry regiments together with a high percentage of mid upper class volunteers. Alexander was killed during a skirmish at Aberdeen, Cape Colony, South Africa.

GEORGE REITH

Grave Text:
'In memory of George Reith secretary & general manager of the Aberdeen and Scottish North-Eastern Railways, and latterly of Clyde Navigation Trust, Glasgow. Born 7th April 1811, died 25th Novr 1889. And his wife Jane Stuart, Born 22nd Sept 1809 died 25th Octr 1899. And of their children: David, died 26 June 1836 aged 13 months. John J Stuart, died 10 March 1843 aged 4 years. Alexander, died 11 Decr 1848 aged 18 months. Joanna, died 16 July 1851 aged 5 months.

James Stuart, died 7 Decr 1853 aged 6 years. And their grandchild Margaret Duncan Low daughter of the Rev. George Duncan Low M.A. born 3rd Feb. 1876 died 11th Dec 1876'.

Situated:
Aberdeen Nellfield Cemetery, Aberdeen, Scotland.

Authors Comment:
A simple but effective memorial to George Reith and his family with his initials on the top in the middle of the date 1889 which is the year of his death. He must have been a very important gentleman in his time going by the appointments which he held. The Scottish North Eastern railway is in fact still open in parts: Perth to Stanley Junction, Kinnaber to Aberdeen, & Brechin to Bridge of Dun. It was formed originally by the amalgamation of the Aberdeen Railway and the Scottish Midland Junction Railway in 1856.

JOHN C MURRAY (JACK)

Grave Text:
'In ever loving memory of our dear child Bella Jeannie Murray who died 28th December 1892 aged 6 years "Safe in the arms of Jesus".
And of my dear husband Alexander Murray who passed away 11th March 1935 aged 74 and of our dear mother Jeannie Gauld beloved and loving wife of the above Alexander Murray who went to join him 19th June 1936 aged 74. Mary E.C. Murray, A.L.C.M. (Polly) daughter of the above who died 6th March 1963 aged 77 adored wife of John C. Murray, (Jack) Master Mariner who died 16th march 1963 aged 76. Capt. Murray was mentioned in Royal Naval despatches and decorated with Lloyds Medal for meritorious service and outstanding

bravery at sea during the First World War.
"I will rest in the port of my god forever, Beyond earths weariness and pain, Behind earths loss eternal gain" '.

Situated:
Aberdeen Nellfield Cemetery, Aberdeen, Scotland.

Authors Comment:
There is a small cross at the top which is the emblem of faith. Quite a prominent memorial to the Murray family. Captain Jack Murray was obviously a very brave man as not only was he mentioned in dispatches (which is no mean feat in its self) but he also was awarded the Lloyds Medal for meritorious service and outstanding bravery at sea. This medal was awarded in silver only 280 times and in bronze 17 times during the First World War. It has a ribbon of one wide vertical white stripe with a light blue narrower stripe either side.

JOHN CARROLL

Grave Text:
'In Memory of John the beloved husband of Margaret Carroll. Died February 27th 1914 aged 54 years. Formally Sergt 4th R.I.Dragn Guards and one of the Corps that went to the relief of General Gordon. This End Was Peace. Also Margaret Carroll the beloved wife of the above Died 8th November 1940 aged 78 years. Resting in Thee'.

Situated:
Sefton Parish Church dedicated to St. Helen, Sefton, Merseyside, England.

Authors Comment:

A quite imposing black marble headstone with ivy leaves around the top signifying immortality and friendship. There is also rope work around the edge.

This grave is found in the churchyard of a very old church which is Grade 1 listed. Sefton Church was first built around 1170 as the private chapel of the Molyneux family. A few stones from that era still exist.

John Carroll was a Sergeant in the 4th Royal Inniskillen Dragoon Guards and as the headstone reminds us was part of the Corps that went to the relief of General Gordon. Gordon had held out for 317 days in Khartoum against the Sudanese rebels lead by The Mahdi but the British relief came two days too late. And as history tells us, General Gordon was killed on 26th January 1885. John Carroll fought at Abu Klea as part of No3 Company on the way to Khartoum on 17th January 1885. When the relief corps returned home they, including John, were personally greeted by Queen Victoria herself.

PETER WINN

Grave Text:
'In Loving Memory of Robert William the beloved husband of Jane Winn, who died 2nd Jany 1925, aged 61 years. Also Peter, son of the above, who lost his life on R.M.S. Lusitania, 7th May 1915, aged 26 years. Also Jane, mother of above, who died 1st Nov. 1949, aged 85 years. "Sleep On" '.

Situated:
Walton Park Cemetery, Walton, Liverpool, England.

Authors Comment:
A nice stone in white with a lovely fringe on the top of flowers and flying insects. The cemetery is now a sanctuary for animals called Rice Lane City Farm, where sheep and other animals roam freely amongst the graves. Peter Winn was a Trimmer on the Lusitania which was torpedoed by the German submarine U-20 on 7th May 1915 killing 1,119 of the 1924 people aboard. Peter was one of those who were killed. The ship left New York on 1st May 1915 bound for Liverpool. At 2.10pm on the 7th, she was sunk off the coast of Ireland and in 18 minutes was under the water. Walter Schwieger was the U boat captain and wrote in his Log: "The ship stops immediately and heals over to starboard quickly, immersing simultaneously at the bow………....". The sinking is thought to have encouraged the Americans into the First World War as the dead included 114 Americans.

HENRY WEBBER

Grave Text:
'Lieutenant Henry Webber, South Lancashire Regt.,
21st July 1916 aged 68.
Of Horsley, Surrey, Dulce et Decorum est Pre Patria Mo...'

Situated:
Dartmoor Commonwealth War Graves Cemetery, Becordel-Becourt, Somme, France.

Authors Comment:
A Commonwealth War Grave headstone made from Portland stone. Currently there are in the region of 20,000 of these headstones made each year and they are all made in the same place, in Arras in France. It displays the badge of the South Lancashire Prince of Wales Volunteers with the words 'Egypt' and "Ich Dien", which means "I serve", on the badge. Henry was a native of Horley, Surrey and had been a member of the London Stock Exchange for over 40 years. On his grave it states he was 68 years old when he died but the Commonwealth War Graves Commission records show him as 67 years old. Henry Webber is the oldest known battle death recorded for the First World War.

I feel sure that this is not a record Henry would have wished for.

ROBERT NOONAN

Grave Text:

'Robert Noonan, 18th April 1870 3rd February 1911 Author as Robert Tressell of "The Ragged Trousered Philanthropists"

"Through squalid life they laboured in sordid grief they died. Those sons of a mighty mother. Those props of England's pride. They are gone. There is none can undo it, Nor save our souls from the curse. But many a million cometh And shall they be better or worse?"

"It is we must answer and hasten and open wide the door.

For the rich man's hurrying terror. And the slow foot hope of the poor." Also Elizabeth Mary Davies, Anna Brown, Margaret Bethell, James Gribb, William Ash, May James, Ann Ashton, William Ducksberry, William Barnes, Mary Davidson, Lilly Harrison, Richard Donald.'

Situated:
Walton Park Cemetery, Walton, Liverpool, England.

Authors Comment:
Robert Noonan was the famous 19th century writer who wrote under the name of 'Robert Tressell'. His book "The Ragged Trousered Philanthropists" was about life in the 1900 house building trade and is a classic novel of humour and characterisation written from a working class perspective. Noonan himself failed to get a publisher in his lifetime and it was his daughter Kathleen who saw her father's book published in 1914. His novel was recently voted 'the most influential book' in a survey of labour MPs in the New Statesman. The headstone you see today was placed there in 1977 as he was buried in a 'public grave' along with twelve other paupers.
It has a nice engraving of Robert Noonan (head and shoulders) on it at the top, along with the names of the other twelve people who share the burial place.

BEATRICE BLORE BROWNE

Grave Text:
'In Loving Memory of Beatrice Blore Browne (Bee) Born September 26th 1887 Died November 23rd 1921 "She feared naught but God".'

Situated:
Great Orme Cemetery, Mynwent, Pen-Y-Gogarth, Llandudno, Conwy, North Wales.

Authors Comment:
What an amazing headstone in white marble. A spoked car wheel with wings. Beatrice was by all accounts a lover of fast cars which for the era was unusual for a lady. In July 1914 the Llandudno Advertiser reported that she had driven a motor car up the Great Orme, presumably prior to it having a road up it as it has today. She was born in Middlesbrough, Yorkshire, England and was one of five children. She was living in Penmaenmawr, North Wales when she died. Quite a lady.

JONATHAN RAWLING

Grave Text:
'Here lieth the Body of Jonathan Rawling late Agent to the old Mine Company at this place who departed this life on the 8th of Decr 1836 Aged 53. This stone was placed as a token of respect by his late Employers. UNDERNEATH Also lieth the remains of Jane Rawling the beloved Wife of the above Jonathan Rawling who departed this life August 3rd 1870 Aged 79 Years'.

Situated:
Great Orme Cemetery, Mynwent, Pen-Y-Gogarth, Llandudno, Conwy, North Wales.

Authors Comment:
Jonathan Rawling must have been a well respected Agent of the Mine for his Employers to pay for a solid blue slate gravestone of this size. There has been a mine on the Great Orme since the Bronze Age. It closed in about 600 BC and was reopened in 1692 where it produced copper until the end of the 19th century. The Great Orme is a rocky piece of headland jutting into the sea and is sized at about two miles long and one mile wide. The word Orme is said to be from the Old Norse word for a sea serpent.

EMMA WYARD

Grave Text:
'In Loving Memory of Emma Wyard
Born 27th Feb: 1857
Died 25th Jan: 1935
A devoted Wife and Mother.'

Situated:
Great Orme Cemetery, Mynwent, Pen-Y-Gogarth, Llandudno, Conwy, North Wales.

Authors Comment:
What a lovely grave this is in white marble.

The statue, which I take to be that of the late Emma Wyard, is extremely lifelike and shows her asleep with her head resting on her hands upon the engraved headstone.

She must have been loved by her family a great deal.

FRANK HORNBY

Grave Text:
'In Sweet Remembrance of Patricia, The dearly loved and only daughter of Frank & Clara Hornby who fell asleep 15th June 1919, in her 14th year. Also of Frank Hornby, father of the above who died September 21st 1936, aged 72 years. Also of Clara Hornby, beloved wife of Frank who died 13th Oct. 1953 aged 92 years.'

Situated:
St Andrews Church, Maghull, Merseyside, England.

Authors Comment:
A Delightful white marble memorial to one of the greatest visionaries in the field of mechanical and engineering toys in the world. It is constructed with a cathedral in mind with its arches, spires and columns. Frank was born 15th May 1863 in Liverpool and after experimenting in his home workshop he began making toys for his sons in 1899. He developed, manufactured and produced three of the most popular toys of the twentieth century: Meccano, Hornby Model Railways, and Dinky Toys. Frank Hornby was also a politician and was elected a Conservative MP for the Everton, Liverpool constituency in 1931. He died in Liverpool on 21st September 1936.

DANIEL DE-FOE

Grave Text:
'Daniel De-Foe. Born 1661. Died 1731. Author of Robinson Crusoe.
This monument is the result of an appeal in the "CHRISTIAN WORLD" newspaper to the boys and girls of England, for funds to place a suitable memorial upon the grave of DANIEL DE-FOE.
It represents the united contributions of seventeen hundred persons Septr 1870.'

Situated:
Bunhill Fields Cemetery, City Road, London, England.

Authors Comment:
This is a tall striking monument which, as the writing states, was erected by subscription by one thousand seven hundred contributors. Daniel was born Daniel Foe and added the "De" to his name later. He was a writer, journalist and a spy. His is best known for his adventure novel "Robinson Crusoe" which he wrote in 1719 which tells the story of a man who survives a shipwreck on a desert island on his own. It is thought that his book was based on a true story of a Scottish castaway, one Alexander Selkirk. De-Foe also spent time in Newgate Prison and from there he was recruited as an intelligence agent.

JOHN BUNYAN

Grave Text:
'John Bunyan, author of the Pilgrims Progress Obt 31st Augt. 1688, Aet. 60.'

Situated:
Bunhill Fields Cemetery, City Road, London, England.

Authors Comment:
This is a magnificent tomb in white marble. It has on the top a statue of Bunyan in repose and on the side a carving of a pilgrim from his famous book.
He was born on 28th November 1628 near Bedford, England. In 1660 he was imprisoned for nearly twelve years for preaching without a licence. It was in the Bedford county gaol that he wrote "Pilgrims Progress". This book is said to be probably the most widely read book in the English language, which has been translated into the most languages with the exception of the Bible.
When released from prison he became a pastor but was rearrested in 1675. He died of a fever on his way to London on 31st August 1688 after catching a very bad cold.

WILLIAM BLAKE

Grave Text:
'Near by lie the remains of the poet-painter William Blake 1757 – 1827 and his wife Catherine Sophia 1762 – 1831.'

Situated:
Bunhill Fields Cemetery, City Road, London, England.

Authors Comment:
A simple headstone. Clear and precise. William Blake was born 28th November 1757 and was a poet, printer and painter. He was largely unrecognised in his lifetime but is now thought to be a significant player in the history of poetry and art.

He attended the Royal Academy in London from 1778.

Blake died on 12th August 1827 and was buried on the eve of his forty-fifth wedding anniversary by Catherine his wife with monies borrowed from John Linnell, a fellow artist.

CHRISTOPHER CONCANON

Grave Text:
'In Memory of Christopher Concanon, Late Governor of H.M.Prison, Walton, Died August 12th 1885, Aged 59 Years. Also of Elizabeth, His Wife, Died April 27th 1921 Aged 86 Years. Also Olivia Concanon, Daughter of above, Died July 3rd 1951, Aged 79 Years.'

Situated:
Walton Park Cemetery, Walton, Liverpool, England.

Authors Comment:
The headstone has a cross which is the emblem of faith and has the symbol IHS, the letters being intertwined and standing for 'In His Service'. Christopher Concanon must have been one of the first Governors of Walton Prison in Liverpool. He must have had an unenviable position but one of power I am sure. It was built between 1850 and 1854 in Hornby Road, Liverpool with an initial capacity of 1,000 inmates. Between 1887 and 1964, 60 men and 2 women suffered the death penalty at the gaol. The first being Elizabeth Berry who was executed on 14th March 1887 for the crime of poisoning her 11 year old daughter for the £10 life insurance money. James Berry, by coincidence was the first executioner and it was he who was Elizabeth Berry's executioner.
Henry Pierrepoint was also an executioner at Walton later on and he executed two people there.

ARTHUR PRICE

Grave Text:
'Arthur Price "Order of St. John" Major R.A.M.C. T.D.
Med. Off. H.M.Prison Walton.
Born June 29. 1853. Died Oct. 16. 1933.'

Situated:
Walton Park Cemetery, Walton, Liverpool, England.

Authors Comment:
Simple grave in the order of a large scroll. Price was a well qualified man with the high army rank of Major in the Royal army Medical Corps. T.D. is the Territorial Decoration which is awarded for long service in the Territorial Force. A minimum of twenty years commissioned service is required for this award.

"The Order of St. John" is a shortened version of the grander title of "The Most Venerable Order of St. John of Jerusalem". It is an order of the British Crown which traces its origins back to the Knights Hospitaller some 900 years ago. It was the Abbey of St. Mary in Jerusalem that set up a hospital to care for sick pilgrims and attached to it was a small church dedicated to St. John.

SIR HIRAM S. MAXIM

Grave Text:
'In Memory of Sir Hiram S. Maxim 1840 – 1916. Lady Sarah Maxim 1854 -1941. Lt Col Maxim Joubert U.S. Army 1902 – 1980.'

Situated:
West Norwood Cemetery, Norwood High Street, London, SE27 9JU, England.

Authors Comment:
This grave has a large grey square stone block as its headstone. Sir Hiram was born on 5th February 1840 in Maine in the USA. He died in London on 24th November 1916. He was an inventor and the most famous invention he made would have to be the first fully automatic, portable machine gun. In contrast he was also the inventor of the common mouse trap.

After immigrating to England in 1881 he was knighted by Queen Victoria in 1901. His machine gun was produced in a factory in Crayford, Kent which was later taken over by the Vickers Company.

JOHN ANDERSON

Grave Text:
'Erected by John Anderson in memory of his beloved mother, Mary Robertson, who died 8th January, 1830, Aged 40.
'Yes! She had friends when fortune smil'd_ it frown'd_ they knew her not! She died the orphans weept_ but liv'd to mark this Hallow'd Spot.' Here, also rests the above John Anderson Wizard Of The North
Died 3rd February 1874 Aged 60.'

Situated:
St. Nicholas Churchyard, Aberdeen, Scotland.

Authors Comment:
A simple white headstone on a plinth but contains strong words.

John Anderson, The Wizard of the North was one of the finest magicians that Scotland ever produced. After starting his working life as an apprentice blacksmith he joined up with a group of travelling players. He made his debut as a magician in Aberdeen in the early 1830's and received his first payment as a magician in 1837. He claimed that the title of 'The Great Wizard of the North' was given to him by Sir Walter Scott who was the original Wizard of the North.

He took his show to America, Canada and most European countries, also to Russia where he is thought to have been one of the first show business acts to perform. He died in Darlington in 1874.

JOHN NICOLL & HELEN WILSON

Grave Text:
'Here are interred the Remains of John Nicoll, late Merchant in Aberdeen, who died in March 1794. And of Helen Wilson his Spoufe, who died in Decemr: 1792. Both in an Advanced Age.
Having by their Settlement of the 26th May 1790. Left Six Hundred and Thirty Pounds of their Property to Public Charities in this City.
Their Executors Caufed this Monument to be Erected as a Tribute due to their Memory.

Situated:
St. Nicholas Churchyard, Aberdeen, Scotland.

Authors Comment:
White marble stone situated in the walls of the churchyard.
The sum left to charities of six hundred and thirty pounds in 1790 would have been quite a sum of money and it is right that their executors saw fit to erect this stone to their memory and state their endowment to Aberdeen's charities.

CHARLES HADDON SPURGEON

Grave Text:
'Here lies the body of Charles Haddon Spurgeon waiting for the appearing of his Lord and Saviour Jesus Christ. Also that of his Dearly Beloved Wife Susannah. " God shall wipe away all the tears from their eyes, And there shall be no more death, Neither sorrow nor crying, Neither shall there be any more pain, For the …. things ………passed away ……." .This

monument was erected in loving memory of C.H.Spurgeon. who was born at Kelvedon, Essex, June 19th 1834, and fell asleep in Jesus at Mentone, France Janry 31st 1892. "For since by faith I saw the stream, thy flowing wounds supply, Redeeming love has been my theme, and shall be till I die, Then in a nobler sweeter song, I'll sing thy power to save, when this poor lisping stammering tongue, lies silent in the grave". In Loving memory of Susannah Spurgeon, born Jan 15 1852, died Oct. 23. 1903. "His love in time past forbids me to think, He'll leave me at last in trouble to link each sweet Ebenezer I have in review Confirms his good pleasure to help me quite through …….. that I meet shall work for my good, the bitter is sweet the memories ……… at present

will ……long and then oh how pleasant the …………".

Situated:
West Norwood Cemetery, Norwood High Street, London, SE27 9JU, England.

Authors Comment:
This is a grand sarcophagus in grey granite with four great pillars holding up the lid. It has a lifelike carving of Spurgeon on the end and has a stone book, presumably the bible, on a cushion that appears ready to be read from by him. Spurgeon was a Reformed Baptist preacher who remains highly influential with Christians of different denominations and is still known as the "Prince of Preachers". His lessons were known to be translated into over thirty languages. He was also an author writing several books. One of Spurgeon sermons was found with missionary David Livingstone's possessions, on which Livingstone had written the comment "Very good D.L.".

JAMES McGRIGOR

Grave Text:
'Sacred to the memory of Lieutenant Colonel James McGrigor. Of the XV Regiment Bombay Native Infantry. Who was drowned at Aden while bathing on the 28th June 1863 AETAT 44.

This tablet was erected by the officers of his regiment as a token of their sincere esteem and regard for him. He was a true Christian, a brave officer, and a kind friend, and was beloved by all who knew him.

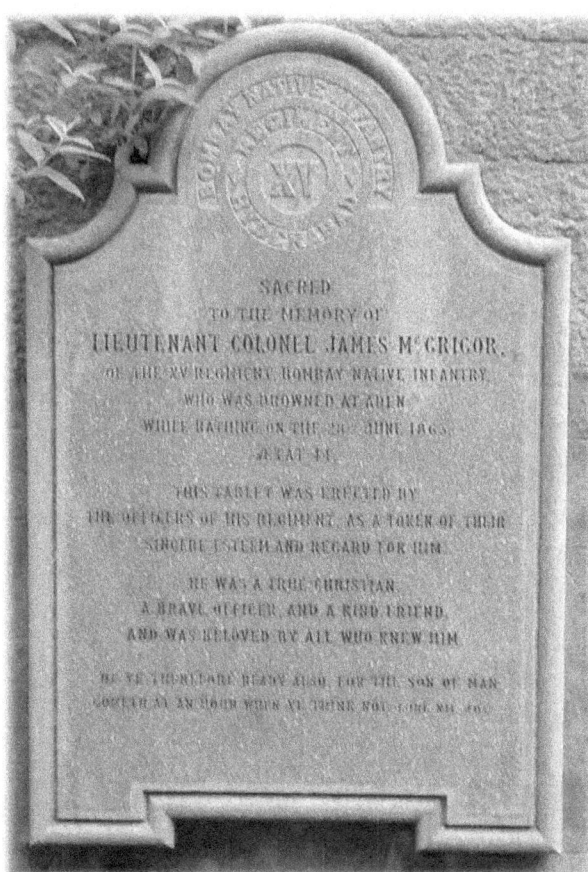

"Be ye therefore ready also: for the Son of man cometh at an hour when ye think not. Luke XII 40v".'

Situated:
St. Nicholas Churchyard, Aberdeen, Scotland.

Authors Comment:
Grey granite plaque erected by the Officers of McGrigor's regiment after his untimely death by drowning. At the top is the crest of the 15th Bombay Native Infantry Regiment which was based in Hyderabad.
The 15th Regiment was formed in 1824 and disbanded in 1882.

CAPTAIN WILLIAM PENNY

Grave Text:
'In memory of Captain William Penny, Aberdeen, Arctic Discoverer who assisted in the Franklin search expedition of 1850 & 1851 and
who died at Aberdeen on 1st Feby 1892 aged 82 years. Also Margaret Irvine wife of Captain William Penny who died at Aberdeen …. June 1901 aged 7.. years ………………'

Situated:
St. Nicholas Churchyard, Aberdeen, Scotland.

Authors Comment:
A magnificent tall Celtic cross which is befitting such an explorer.
It has an anchor which relates to the fact that he was of a seafaring profession and at the top a carved whale. The whale is a reference to the fact that William Penny was an Aberdeen whaling master who had been given a naval commission and was the commander of the first steam whaler into the Arctic. He played a major role in the search for Sir John Franklin and the crew of the 'Erebus' and 'Terror' who became lost in the Arctic in an attempt to locate the Northwest Passage. Penny sailed in 1850 and found traces of Franklin's winter quarters of 1845-46 on Beechey Island, but not the 129 officers and men of the lost expedition. Penny did find three graves from the fated expedition.

SIR HENRY TATE

Grave Text:
'Family Vault of Henry Tate.
Until the day dawns and the shadows flee away.'

Situated:
West Norwood Cemetery, Norwood High Street, London, SE27 9JU, England.

Authors Comment:
This grand mausoleum was built by Harold Peto who also was architect for the mausoleum of Sir Henry Doulton. It was built using a combination of effects achieved by red terracotta tiles with alternating buff banding. There are two trumpets bearing Pre-Raphaelite angels either side of the window apertures with gold and silver leaf adorning the vaulted ceiling.
Trumpeting angels stand for resurrection, the angel being the messenger between God and man.
Sir Henry Tate was the founder of Tate & Lyle and was the inventor of the sugar cube. He built the Tate Gallery (1897) in London on the site of the old Millbank Prison and donated his entire art collection to the nation to be displayed there. He was born 11th March 1819 in Chorley, Lancashire and died in London on December 5th 1899. During his lifetime he made many donations, some anonymously. Donations were known to be made to; Liverpool University, Streatham Library, Hahnemann Hospital in Liverpool, a library at Manchester College in Oxford and many more.

THE REMAINS OF AN UNKNOWN AUSTRALIAN SOLDIER

Grave Text:
'The remains of an unknown Australian soldier lay in this grave for 75 years. On 2nd November 1993 they were exhumed and now rest in the Tomb of the Unknown Australian Soldier at the Australian War Memorial in Canberra.'

Situated: Adelaide War Cemetery, Villers-Bretonneux, Somme, France.

Authors Comment: The Australian War Memorial was opened in Canberra in 1941 and overlooks Parliament House. It is considered one of Australia's greatest memorials and stands it the top of Anzac parade. It is the home to a large collection of pictures, media and information about the War and also holds personal and public records.

There is a wreath laying ceremony held every week on the Tomb of the Unknown Australian soldier.

JOHN BONNAR

Grave Text:
'In loving memory of John Bonnar, charabanc owner, Aberdeen who died on the 9th of July 1926 aged 52 years. His wife Diana died on the 16th of July 1949.
Also their son-in-law Hunter McLeod Will died on the 18th of February 1966 aged 80 years. And his wife Diana Bonnar died on the 5th of January 1983 aged 75 years. Also her twin brother John Bonnar died on the 20th of June 1987 aged 80 years. Thy Will Be Done.'

Situated:
Allenvale Cemetery, Aberdeen, Scotland.

Authors Comment:
Large memorial with a cross near the top, the emblem of faith. John Bonnar was a charabanc owner and was I think well known for this in the area. A charabanc is an open-topped bus which was common in the early part of the 20th century. The name derives from the French 'char a bancs' (a carriage with wooden benches) where the vehicle originated in the 20th century.

The original charabanc in Britain was a horse-drawn vehicle which was normally open and had several rows of seats across its width. The charabancs where particularly popular for 'works' outings where they took their employees to the country or the seaside once a year for a day trip.

SIR HENRY DOULTON

Grave Text:
'Family Vault of Sir Henry Doulton. "He discovereth deep things out of darkness, and bringeth out to light the shadow of death.".'

Situated:
West Norwood Cemetery, Norwood High Street, London, SE27 9JU, England.

Authors Comment:
This is a lovely structure designed by Architect Harold Peto who had just completed building the Doulton's country house 'Woolpits' in Surrey. The structure was built using Doulton's own terracotta blocks and miniature bricks with a crenellation separating the terracotta roof. There are several crosses on the structure, one appears to be Celtic and it also has a Jewish star carved on it, beneath the text.

Henry Doulton was born 25th July 1820 in Vauxhall, one of eight children of pottery manufacturer John Doulton. He joined the family business in 1835 and was instrumental in developing the firm of 'Royal Doulton'. In 1887 Henry Doulton was knighted and also received the Albert Medal by the Royal Society of Arts a few years later. He died on the 18th November 1897.

FRANK W. McDONALD & J. M. McDONALD

Grave Text:
'Erected by J. M. McDonald, Slater, Aberdeen in loving memory of his sons Gunner Frank W. McDonald, R. F. A. aged 27 years, Wounded at the Somme July 9th 1916 and died at Hemel-Hempstead, Herts September 28th 1916, on his way back to France. Sgt. J. M. McDonald, R.A.M.C. died at Stobs Military Hospital Hawick 11th August 1920 aged

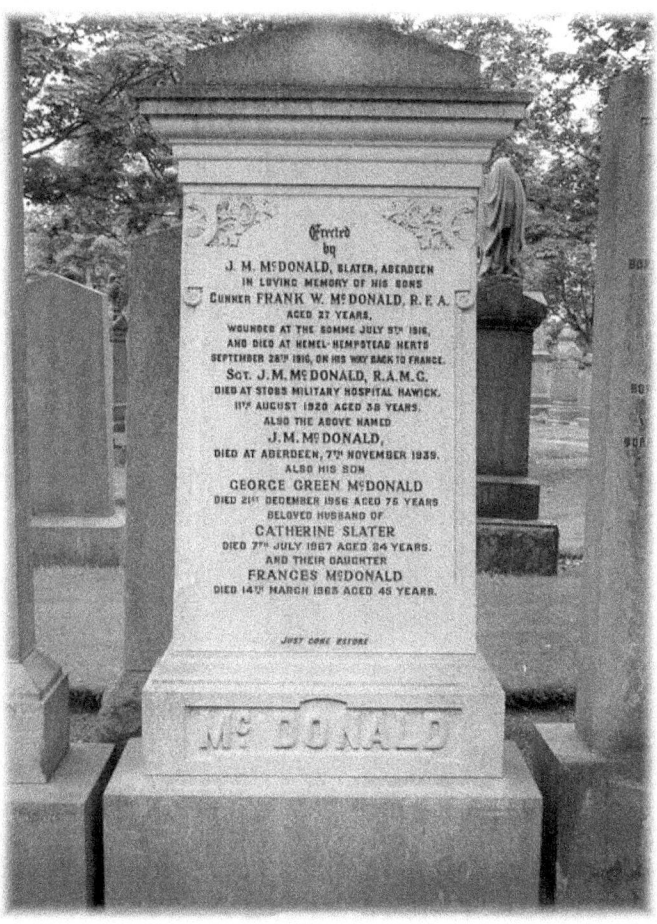

38 years. Also the above named J. M. McDonald died at Aberdeen 7th November 1939. Also his son George Green McDonald died 21st December 1956 aged 75 years. Beloved husband of Catherine Slater died 7th July 1967 aged 84 years.

And their daughter Frances McDonald died 14th March 1963 aged 45 years. Just Come Before.'

Situated:
Allenvale Cemetery, Aberdeen, Scotland.

Authors Comment:
Substantial grey stone memorial with the name McDonald in large letters near the base. It is sad that two of the sons of J. M. McDonald should die during the First World War but this was unfortunately a common fact of the war. Frank was a driver in the Royal Field Artillery, 49th Reserve Battery and according to the grave text was killed on his way back to France after being wounded in the Battle of the Somme in 1916. James was a Quartermaster Sergeant in the Royal Medical Corps. 13th Company, and he died at a Scottish military hospital in 1920, two years after the official end of the war.

JOHN SCOTT RIDDELL

Grave Text:
'In Memory of John Scott Riddell M.A., M.B., G.M., M.V.O., C.B.E., T.D., LL.D., D.L., Knight of Grace of the Order of St. John of Jerusalem. Surgeon to the Aberdeen Royal Infirmary. 1891 – 1919. Hon, Colonel R.M.A.C. (T.), Red Cross Commissioner for the North Eastern District of Scotland during the Great War 1914 – 1919. Born April 10th 1864. Entered into rest December 3rd 1929. And his beloved wife Jeanie Grindlay Scott Riddell. Born October 1st 1874, departed this life March 25th 1960.'

Situated:
Allenvale Cemetery, Aberdeen, Scotland.

Authors Comment:
Large stone-like memorial with a large cross carved near the top, the emblem of faith, and a Maltese cross near the plinth signifying the connection of John Scott Riddell to the Order of St. John. This gentleman had a wealth of awards and was recognised in many ways judging from the letters after his name. From the grave text it shows that he had been awarded the C.B.E. This medal is part of the Most Excellent Order of the British Empire which was established in 1917 by King George V. The Order includes five classes in civil and military divisions. The letters C.B.E. stand for 'Commander of the British Empire'.

WILLIAM BLIGH

Grave Text:
'Sacred to the memory of William Bligh Esquire, F. R. S., Vice Admiral of the Blue. The celebrated navigator who first transplanted the bread fruit tree from Otaheite to the West Indies. Bravely fought the battles of his country and died beloved, respected, and lamented on the 7th day of December 1817, aged 64. Sacred to the memory of Mrs Elizabeth Bligh the wife of Rear Admiral Bligh who died April 15th 1812 in the 60 year of her age. Her spirit soar'd to heav'n. The blest domain where virtue only can its meed obtain. All the great

duties she perform'd thro' life. Those of a child, a parent, and a wife. In this vault are deposited also the remains of William Bligh and Henry Bligh who died March 21 1795 aged 1 day, the sons of M. Elizabeth and Rear Admiral Bligh; and also Wm. Bligh Barker, their grandchild, who died Oct 22nd 1805 aged 3 years.'

Situated:
St. Mary's Lambeth, London, England.

Authors Comment:
A noble monument to a noble gentleman to whom history may not have been so kind. A white stone memorial with a large urn on the top. Around the sarcophagus are a number of carvings: wreaths, meaning victory; coat of arms; scallop shells, meaning resurrection; and scrolls. Bligh is generally remembered in history as Captain Bligh and the Mutiny on the Bounty that occurred against his command and the remarkable voyage he made to Timor after being set adrift by the mutineers. Many years after the mutiny he was appointed Governor of New South Wales with a brief to clean up the corrupt rum trade.

He was born in Plymouth in 1754 and signed up to the Royal Navy in 1761 then aged 7 years. In 1776 he was selected by Captain James Cook to be Sailing Master of the 'Resolution' and accompanied Cook in July of that year on Cook's third and fatal voyage to the Pacific. In 1787 Bligh took command of The Bounty and set sail for Tahiti to obtain Breadfruit trees. He was taking them to the Caribbean when the mutiny occurred. In 1790 Bligh was honourably acquitted at the court-marshal into the loss of The Bounty. Three of the mutineers were convicted of mutiny and were hanged.

JAMES SCOTT SKINNER

Grave Text:
'James Scott Skinner 1843 1927. 'The Bonnie Lass O' Bon-Accord'
In Memory of James Scott Skinner "The Strathspey King".
Born at Banchory 15th August 1843 – Died Aberdeen 17th March 1927.
The Greatest Violin Exponent & Composer of Scottish National Music.
Erected by his many Friends and Admirers.'

Situated:
Allenvale Cemetery, Aberdeen, Scotland.

Authors Comment:
This is a very striking memorial in white marble with a bust of Skinner in an alcove. It also has a carved violin and bow and the 'score' from 'The Bonnie Lass O'Bon-Accord'.

James Scott Skinner was a Scottish violinist and fiddler who was also a Scottish dancing master.

His father was also a dancing master but died when James was only eighteen months old. His brother taught him the violin. He went to Connell's School in Aberdeen and three years later in 1855 he joined "Dr Mark's Little Men" who were a travelling orchestra. The orchestra performed in front of Queen Victoria at Buckingham Palace in 1858. Over 600 of his compositions were published and the best known of these is the one on his monument.

E. McGARVIE

Grave Text:
'7393195 Private E. McGarvie, Royal Army Medical Corps. 22nd August 1943.'

Situated:
Kanchanaburi War Cemetery, Thailand.

Authors Comment:
The headstones in Kanchanaburi War Cemetery are quite small and are laid flat on the ground due to the ground being quite wet for most of the year. It is situated 129 kilometres north-west of Bangkok. The notorious Burma-Siam railway was a Japanese army project during WW II in Burma and approximately 13,000 prisoners of war died building it. The legendary Bridge over the River Kwai was part of this stretch of railway.

Private McGarvie was in the Royal Army Medical Corps.  The R.A.M.C is a specialist Corps providing medical services to the British Army and their families in war and peace. The badge of the Corps has a serpent on it and the motto of 'In Arduis Fidelis' meaning 'Faithful in Adversity'. It was founded under its present name in 1898 but its roots go back as far as 1660.

CEDRIC CHARLES DICKENS

Grave Text:
'In loving memory of our darling Ceddy. Major Cedric Charles Dickens, 1/13th Kensington Btn. The London Regiment. Born 8th March 1889, killed in Action Leuze Wood 9th Sept1916. RIP'.

Situated:
Leuze Wood, Somme, France.

Authors Comment:
Major Dickens was the grandson of the famous writer Charles Dickens. This simple wooden cross marks the spot where he was killed on 9th September 1916. His body was never found and he is remembered also on the Thiepval Memorial. Leuze Wood its self no longer exists. Some of Charles Dickens's novels were: The Pickwick Papers, The Adventures of Oliver Twist, David Copperfield, A Christmas Carol, and The Old Curiosity Shop, to mention but a few.

ANTHONY TROLLOPE

Grave Text:
'In memory of Anthony Trollope, born 24th April 1815, died 6th December 1882, He was a loving husband, a loving father, and a true friend.
"Into thy hand I commit my soul" '.

Situated:
Kensal Green Cemetery, Harrow Road, London, W10 4RA, England.

Authors Comment:
A solid pink granite ledger with a raised cross on the top. This is on top of a grey granite base. Anthony Trollope was an English novelist who's best loved writings were known as the Chronicles of Barsetshire. They were known as this because they revolve around the imaginary English county of Barsetshire.

He wrote a total of 47 novels and a number of short stories. Trollope spent his working life in the Post Office and his most lasting memorial is the fact that he introduced the pillar-box to the United Kingdom. This bright red mail-box that adorns the British high street.

CATHERINE JONES

Grave Text:
'Catherine Dautr of John Jones, Coachman by Susan his wife Buried June 15th 1813'.

Situated:
St Mael & St Sulien (Corwen Parish Church) Corwen, Denbyshire, Wales.

Authors Comment:
A small and simple headstone which has kept well over the past near two hundred years. It is interesting that the stone mason has carved the word dautr with the 'tr' raised above the writing level as is the 's' of Jones and the 'th' of the 15th. There are two shining suns, one in each top corner which

signifies life everlasting. There is also a leaf hanging down in the top middle and this means regeneration and immortality.
Catherine's father John Jones was a Coachman and one can picture him driving his coach and four horses with his cape trailing in the wind behind him.

Dr Henry John Gauntlett

Grave Text:
'In loving memory of Henry John Gauntlett church musician Born at Olney, Bucks, 1805. Died in Kensington 1876.
Also of Henrietta Gipps widow of the above, Born 1819 Died 1891. Also of Henry Vivian Deane son of H C D Gauntlett and grandson of the above Born Oct 6 1882 Died July 16 1893, Also of Henry Chrysostom Deane eldest son of the above Henry John Gauntlett Born 2 March 1847. Died 27 October 1924 and of his wife Catherine Gauntlett at rest Dec 4 1935 aged 77'.

Situated:
Kensal Green Cemetery, Harrow Road, London, W10 4RA, England.

Authors Comment:
A rather weathered headstone with a carving of the intertwined letters IHS, standing for "In His Service". He became the organist at his father's church in Olney when he was only nine years of age. Dr Henry Gauntlett was an organist and songwriter who's most famous contribution to music was the tune called "Irby" to which the hymn "Once in Royal David's City" is sung. He wrote in excess of one thousand hymn tunes in his lifetime.

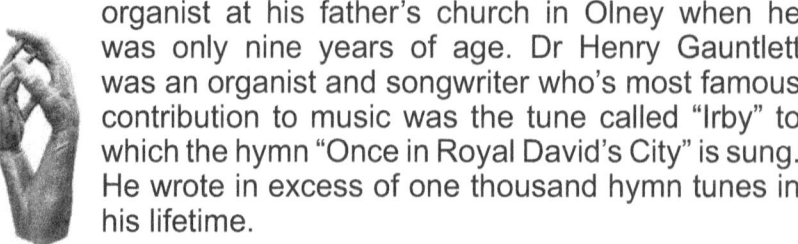

CATHERINE EDWARDS

Grave Text:
'Sacred to the memory of Catherine Edwards wife of David Edwards Lower Street in this town Died June 29th 1856 aged 59 years ....Margaret ....'

Situated:
St Myllin's Church, Llanfyllin, Powys, Wales.

Authors Comment:
This gravestone is in excellent condition and the writing is very crisp and clear. It has two shining suns at the top, meaning life everlasting, and a smaller carving on the top centre. The fascinating thing about this headstone is the writings on it which are written in the Theban alphabet and one wonders if it was written in order to conceal the inscription. The Theban alphabet was written many years ago and its origins have been lost to time. It was first published in Johannes Trithemius' "Polygraphia" in 1518. It is also known as the Honorian Alphabet or the Runes of Honorian., and the Witches' Alphabet. There is a one to one correspondence between letters of the Theban and Latin alphabets with the exception of the letters J and U which are represented by the letters I and V. It has a quite mystical quality.

WILLIAM HENRY SMITH

Grave Text:
'Sacred to the memory of Clara Smith, sixth daughter of W. H. Smith Esq' who died on the 14th day of September 1839 aged 8 years. Also of Mrs Elizabeth Cooper grandmother of the above who died on the 4th day June 18..0 in the 75th year of her age. Also of Mary Ann the beloved wife of W. H. Smith Esq' who died on the 17th day of March 18.... Aged 59 years.

Also to the memory of William Henry Smith Esquire who died on the 28th day of July 1865 aged 73 years. The path of the just is as the shining light ......, shineth more and more unto the perfect day. Also of Henry Walton Danvers son of W. H. Smith Esquire and grandson of the above who died on the 7th day of Feby 1..... aged 4 months and 6 days.'

Situated:
Kensal Green Cemetery, Harrow Road, London, W10 4RA, England.

Authors Comment:
A chest tomb with a grey granite base and a bright pink granite top. On the top is a stone book which looks as if someone has left it open whilst they read it. The stone book is befitting William Henry Smith or W. H. Smith as the newsagent and bookshops are known today. He was an entrepreneur with businesses in both book shops and newsagents. He found success in the family business and had outlets at London's railway stations. The W. H. Smith as we see today has its roots back in 1790 when Henry Everett and William Smith founded a news agency service for the public. In 1792 Henry Walton Smith and his wife Anna established W. H. Smith as a news vendor in London.

William Henry Smith took over after the deaths of his parents Henry and Anna in 1812, and when his son William Henry became a partner in 1846 the firm became W. H. Smith & Son.

HENRY AND JOHN JONES

Grave Text:
'Er cof am anwyl blant David a Mary Jones Pen y Bont Fawr
Henry yr hwn a fu farw Ebrill 30ain 1884 yn 10 mis oed
A John yr hwn a fu farw Mai 17fed 1886 yn 10 mis oed
Ac a gladdwyd yn mynwent Pen y Bont Fawr.'
Translated to English:
In memory of the dear children of David and Mary Jones Pen y Bont Fawr. Henry who died April 30th 1884 aged 10 months and John who died May 17th 1886 aged 10 months and are buried in the cemetery Pen y Bont Fawr.

Situated:
St Thomas' Church, Penybontfawr, Powys, Wales.

Authors Comment:
A small wooden headstone which is over one hundred and twenty years old. It is not common to see a wooden headstone in a cemetery as they do not tend to last long due to the action of weather on the material used. This one has lasted very well and the text is still legible. Even the thin edge trimmings are in place and you can see the nails which attach the edging. It has a cross carved at the top. David Jones was a carpenter by trade, and not being a rich man would probably have carved the headstone himself. It is such a shame that David and Mary Jones should loose two children both when they were ten months old but the death rate for children was much greater in those days than it is now. They went on to have four more children, three of whom lived to their 80's and one who died aged only five months.

GUDMUNDUR THORSTEINSSON (MUGGUR)

Grave Text:
'G.Th. Gudmundur Thorsteinsson Malari 1891 1924.'

Situated:
Holavallagardur Cemetery, Reykjavik, Iceland.

Authors Comment:
This is a most beautiful headstone which has a colourful mosaic by Elof Risebye who was a professor at the Royal Danish Academy of Fine Art.

Gudmundur was himself a painter and on the stone below the mosaic are his initials 'G. Th.' as they appear on his paintings.

He was known as 'Muggar' and was not just a painter but was also a film actor. As a painter he worked in water colours, oil, charcoal and collages.

He died on the 26th July 1924 from tuberculosis aged 32.

JEAN FRANCOIS GRAVELET-BLONDIN

Grave Text:
'In memory of my beloved wife Charlotte Gravelet Blondin who died 15th December 1888 aged 52.
In loving memory of Katherine Gravelet Blondin died July 13th 1901 aged 36 years.
In memory of Jean Francois Gravelet Blondin who died at Niagra House Ealing 22nd February 1897 in his 73rd year.'

Situated:
Kensal Green Cemetery, Harrow Road, London, W10 4RA, England.

Authors Comment:
This is a most handsome monument to one of the greatest tightrope walkers of all time. It is made from pink Peterhead granite on a black base and has the portraits of both the artist and his wife. There is a large marble Romanesque figure adorning the top and has IHS (In His Service) engraved between the portraits. The whole memorial is surrounded by a low black wall with pink granite posts which originally would have had some sort of chain linking them. Jean Francois Gravelet Blondin was known by a number of names, Charles Blondin, Emile Blondin, and The Great Blondin. He was born at St Omer in France and went to the Ecole de Gymnase at Lyon when he was only five years old.

Blondin is famously known for the crossing of Niagra Falls on a tightrope and in fact carried his manager Harry Colcord across on his back.

He also crossed Niagra Falls in a sack, with a wheelbarrow, on stilts, blindfolded, and once he stopped halfway and fried and ate an omelette. He even named his house in Ealing, Niagra House.

SIGURDUR BREIDFJORD

Grave Text:
'Sigurdur Breidfjord 1799 – 1846.'

Situated:
Holavallagardur Cemetery, Reykjavik, Iceland.

Authors Comment:
This gravestone is in the shape of a triangle with what looks like a harp shape carved above the text. It is made from a light coloured stone.
It was carved by stonemason Svernir Runolfsson who has other gravestones to his name in the cemetery. He trained in Denmark.
Sigurdur was an Icelandic poet who prior to this had trained as a cooper in Copenhagen and worked in this trade in Iceland and Greenland.
He was a traditional poet known for his 'Rimur' cycles (a Rimur is an epic poem which is rhymed and consists of two to four lines per stanza) . His best known work was 'Numar Rimur'.

JOSEPH LOCKE

Grave Text:
'Joseph Locke, Civil Engineer, born 9 August 1805, died 18 September 1860. Phoebe widow of Joseph Locke and daughter of John and Phoebe McCreery died 15 December 1866. Erected by his pupils in token of their esteem and affectionate regard in 1862.
To the memory of John McCreery, born at Burndennet near Strabane County Tyrone Ireland died in Paris April 18th 1832 aged 65 years.
Also to the memory of Phoebe McCreery his wife who died at Richmond Surrey 20th May 1849.
Enlarged and restored in 1870 by Sarah McCreery.'

Situated:
Kensal Green Cemetery, Harrow Road, London, W10 4RA, England.

Authors Comment:
Grand Pink Peterhead Granite and Grey Irish Granite plinth. Has pillars and a forefront. The McCreery tomb has a scrolled top and an hourglass on the front representing 'the passing of time'.

Joseph Locke was a civil engineer who was noted for his railway projects in England, France, Spain and Holland. He worked with Stephenson on the Manchester and Liverpool Railway. He is ranked alongside both Stephenson and Isambard Kingdom Brunel in relation to their railway development pioneering.

In later life he was a Liberal Member of Parliament. Locke Park in Barnsley was dedicated to his life by his widow Phoebe and it has a statue of him within the park. He died apparently from appendicitis whilst on a shooting holiday.

PORDUR PAISSON

Grave Text:
'Pordur Paisson Hjeraoslaeknin f 30 juni 1876 d 24 des 1922.'

Situated:
Holavallagardur Cemetery, Reykjavik, Iceland.

Authors Comment:
An attractive memorial to Pordur Paisson who was a District Doctor. It is a column of white marble on an ionic base and is covered by a veil of sorrow. A tradition throughout Europe was such that a black cloth was placed over statues or pictures when people died, since such objects represent the world of time that the deceased has left.

The column is a symbol of life and by veiling it, it represents the end of what it was.

CHARLES BABBAGE

Grave Text:
'Charles Babbage Esq Born 22 December 1791 died 18 October 1871.'

Situated:
Kensal Green Cemetery, Harrow Road, London, W10 4RA, England.

Authors Comment:
A grey Aberdeen Granite tomb. Very neat with still sharp edges. Charles Babbage is regarded as one of the greatest mathematicians ever. He was the first person to construct a logarithm table and his passion was the construction of a calculating machine. He was the first person to come up with an idea of a programmable computer, so you could argue that he was the father of the computer age. In order to assist in his idea he was given a grant of £17,000 by the British Government.
He was also a philosopher and a mechanical engineer.
Apparently Babbage's brain is preserved within the Science Museum in London.

SIGFUS EINARSSON

Grave Text:
'Sigfus Einarsson Tonskald F30.Januar 1877 – D.10.Mai 1939 og kona hans Valborg Einarsson F.2.Mai 1883 – D.24. Juli 1969.'

Situated:
Holavallagardur Cemetery, Reykjavik, Iceland.

Authors Comment:
This is a tall stone 'pillar' with a bronze plaque bearing the text and above this the face of Sigfus Einarsson on a bank of organ pipes.
It is well designed and stands out against some of the other surrounding graves.
He was a classical musician and composer and wrote works also for the male voice choir.

Col. Frederick Robertson Aikman V.C.

Grave Text:
'The Family Mausoleum of Capt George Robertson Aikman of the Hon E.I.Companys service of Ross and Bromelton Lanarkshire and of …….. and of…………. London, Ano Domini 1844. And of Frederick their 6th son born 6th Feb 1828 died 5th Oct 1888 served through the Indian Mutiny and was awarded the Victoria Cross, and of William their fourth son born 12th Mar 1822 died 15th Oct 190.. and of Georgina their eldest daughter born 1st Dec 1815 and died 16th Mar 1904. and of Sarah Eliza their youngest daughter born 6th Dec 1829 died 8th Sep 1913.'

Situated:
Kensal Green Cemetery, Harrow Road, London, W10 4RA, England.

Authors Comment:
A rather weathered Portland Stone Mausoleum with columns at the front and their family coat of arms above the first inscription. It also has wreaths all around the top beneath the

roof. It has five steps up to it. Frederick Robertson Aikman was a Scottish recipient of the Victoria Cross which he earned for bravery whilst serving during the Indian Mutiny on 1st March 1858 when he was 30 years of age. He was a lieutenant in the 4th Bengal Native Infantry and the citation reads as follows:

"This Officer, Commanding the 3rd Sikh Cavalry on the advanced Picquet, with one hundred of his men, having obtained information, just as the Force marched on the morning of the 1st March last, of the proximity, three miles off the high road, of a body of 500 Rebel Infantry, 200 Horse, and 2 Guns, under Moosahib Ali Chuckbdar, attacked and utterly routed them, cutting up more than 100 men, capturing two guns, and driving the survivors into, and over, the Goomtee. This feat was performed under every disadvantage of broken ground, and partially under the flanking fire of an adjoining Fort. Lieutenant Aikman received a severe sabre cut in the face in a personal encounter with several of the enemy". We can see from the citation that he was truly a heroic figure.

He ended his military career as a colonel.

ERLENDUR GUOMUNDSSON

Grave Text:
'Erlendur Guomundsson ....1892.'

Situated:
Holavallagardur Cemetery, Reykjavik, Iceland.

Authors Comment:
This delightful monument is one of only a few in the cemetery which are actual works of art.
It has an appearance similar to that of the statues which are found on Easter Island and is carved from stone.
The title is "Finngalk" and it was made by sculptor Sigurjon Olafsson. Surrounding the plot are found stones from the seashore laid by painter Porvaldur Skulason and Sigunjon Olafsson. Painter Nina Tryggvadottir is said to have been behind the memorial.

WILLIAM POTTS

Grave Text:
'In memory of William Potts Esqr of this city late Major in the 8th Regt of Foot who died J... 21st 1821 aged 84 years also of Annie his wife who died Decr 29th 1836 aged 62 years.'

Situated:
St Cuthbert's with St Mary Parish Church, Carlisle, Cumbria, England.

Authors Comment:

A headstone which is presently on the side wall of the church. It is of sandstone which accounts for its poor condition as it is over 180 years old.

As it states, William Potts had been a Major in the 8th Regiment of Foot which is a Regiment which sees its origins in the Princess Anne of Denmark's Regiment of Foot which starts back in 1685. It became the 8th Regiment of Foot in 1751 and is part of the King's Regiment.

The Regiment saw action in the Battle of the Boyne in 1690 and in the Jacobite Rebellions and the Seven Years War both in the 1700's.

Other action came in the American Revolutionary War, The French Revolutionary War and the Napoleonic Wars.

In 1846 the Regiment made it's way to Bombay, India and when the Indian Mutiny began in 1857 they fought in this also.

In 1881 they were renamed The King's (Liverpool Regiment) and in 1921 The King's Regiment (Liverpool).

GUDJON SIGURDSSON

Grave Text:
'Gudjon Sigurdsson ursmidur 1864 – 1915.'

Situated:
Holavallagardur Cemetery, Reykjavik, Iceland.

Authors Comment:
A most unusual memorial which appears to be made from pink granite and has the appearance of having tree roots at the bottom above a small plinth base.
The text plaque and above it the head of Gudjon Sigurdsson in a metal which could be bronze or copper.
There is not much text on this or any of the other graves in this cemetery which appears to be the custom in Iceland. Normally just the deceased persons name and the year they were born and died.

THOMAS SIMPSON

Grave Text:
'To the memory of Thomas Simpson, forty one years Civil Engineer of Chelsea Water-Works, London. By his skill and perseverance along with his celebrated associates Watt and Rennie, he greatly contributed to raise their professions to that eminence which it has so justly obtained throughout Europe. He was the original projector of Lambeth Water-Works and the cities of London and Westminster together with Glasgow and Liverpool are equally benefited by his scientific knowledge. He was born at Blackwell in the parish and died at Chelsea, much and deservedly respected April 24th 1823 in the 68th year of his age.'

Situated:
St Cuthbert's with St Mary Parish Church, Carlisle, Cumbria, England.

Authors Comment:
A white marble plaque inside the foyer of the church. It has four roses, two at the top and two at the bottom signifying silence or perfection. It has two lions heads at the top, one each side, signifying courage. A sheath of corn is in the centre at the very top meaning ripe old age.

The Chelsea Waterworks Company was established in 1723 and received a Royal Charter on 8th March that year. Under James Simpson (Thomas's son) it became the first in the country to install a slow sand filtration system to purify water from the River Thames. This filter consisted of successive beds of loose brick, gravel and sand to remove solids from the water. James had followed his father Thomas in both his post of engineer of Lambeth Water Company and of Chelsea Waterworks.

WILLIAM WORDSWORTH

Grave Text:

'…………….. of Sarah Hutchison the beloved sister and ……… friend who …. caused this stone to be erected with an earnest wish that their own remains may be laid by her side and a …… hope the through Christ they may together be made ….. of the same blessed resurrection. She was born at Penrith ….. Jany 1775 and died at Rydal 23rd June 1835. In fulfilment of the wish are now gathered near here the

remains of: William Wordsworth born Cockermouth 7th April 1770. Died Rydal 23rd April 1850. And of Dorothy Wordsworth born Cockermouth 25th December 177.. died at Rydal 25th January 1855. And finally Mary Wordsworth Wife of William Wordsworth and sister of Sarah Hutchinson born at Penrith August 16th 1770 died at Rydal Mount, January 17th 1859.'

Situated:
St Oswald's Church, Grasmere, Cumbria, England.

Authors Comment:
William Wordsworth was an acclaimed poet and described Grasmere as "The fairest place on Earth". He was born 7th April 1770 in Cockermouth, Cumberland, the second of five children and died 23rd April 1850 at Rydal Mount. William went to Hawkshead Grammar School after the death of his mother in 1778. In 1787 he attended St John's College, Cambridge. His first poetry publications were the collections of "An Evening Walk" and "Descriptive Sketches" in 1793. In 1843 he became Poet Laureate but when his daughter Dora died in 1847 he stopped writing. Wordsworth's most famous poem is now "I wandered lonely as a cloud". The first verse goes as follows:

"I wandered lonely as a cloud
That floats on high o'er vales and hills,
When all at once I saw a crowd,
A host, of golden daffodils;
Beside the lake, beneath the trees,
Fluttering and dancing in the breeze."

HANNES HAFSTEIN

Grave Text:
'Hannes Hafstein 4 Desember 1861 - 13 Desember 1922.
Fru Ragnheidur Hafstein 3. April 1871 18. Juli 1913.'

Situated:
Holavallagardur Cemetery, Reykjavik, Iceland.

Authors Comment:
There are two separate memorials one for Hannes Hafstein and one for his wife Ragnheidur Haftstein. They are both gleaming black granite columns (representing life, its continuation and glory and the human journey cut short by a swift blow) broken diagonally on a large base. These are surrounded by ornate black metal railings with two small gates to the side.

The column of Hannes has an image of Christ, made from copper and is by Einar Jonsson who created it in various forms under the title "Komid til min" (Come to me). Ragnheidur's column, also by Einar entitled "Morgunrodinn" (Dawn).

Hannes Hafstein was Prime Minister of Iceland and a writer.

JANE ATKINSON

Grave Text:
'Here lies the body of Jane Atkinson relict of Mr Thos Atkinson of Upper Cark and oldest daughter of Mr John Marshall of Aynsom who died Octr the 3rd 1760 aged 73.'

Situated:
The Priory Church of St Mary & St Michael, Cartmel, Cumbria, England.

Authors Comment:
This gravestone is situated within the Priory as part of the floor, although it may not have started life there. It has a skull and crossbones at the top signifying 'death' and a winged hourglass just beneath this signifying 'time flying'. Although it is made from stone it has a bronzed look presumably due to ageing. It is very old at 240 plus years and would make Jane's birth around 1687 which was the year that Isaac Newton's Philosophiae Naturalis Principia Mathematics was published.

GUDRIDUR MAGNUSDOTTIR

Grave Text:
' Hjer Hviler Liosmosir, Gudridur Magnusdottir ....
22 April 1801 – Dain 23 April 1864.'

Situated:
Holavallagardur Cemetery, Reykjavik, Iceland.

Authors Comment:
A cast-iron cross on the grave of midwife Gudridur Magnusdottir. This cross, which is a common site in Icelandic cemeteries has a number of symbols on it.

It has an extinguished torch and an hour glass representing 'death'. Palm leaves for 'victory over death', and clasped hands for 'friendship and reunion'. The three ends of the cross are shaped like a bird's head with its two eyes and its head dressed plume.

JANE KELLET

Grave Text:
'Jane Kellet of Weltenhow by Will gave the interest of 45:(& also of 100: More after the deceafe of Iohn Kellet her brother dying without ifsue) to poor of this parish, yearly for ever;& was buryed near this place the tenth day of Jan: Anno D: 1708 aged 22.'

Situated:
The Priory Church of St Mary & St Michael, Cartmel, Cumbria, England.

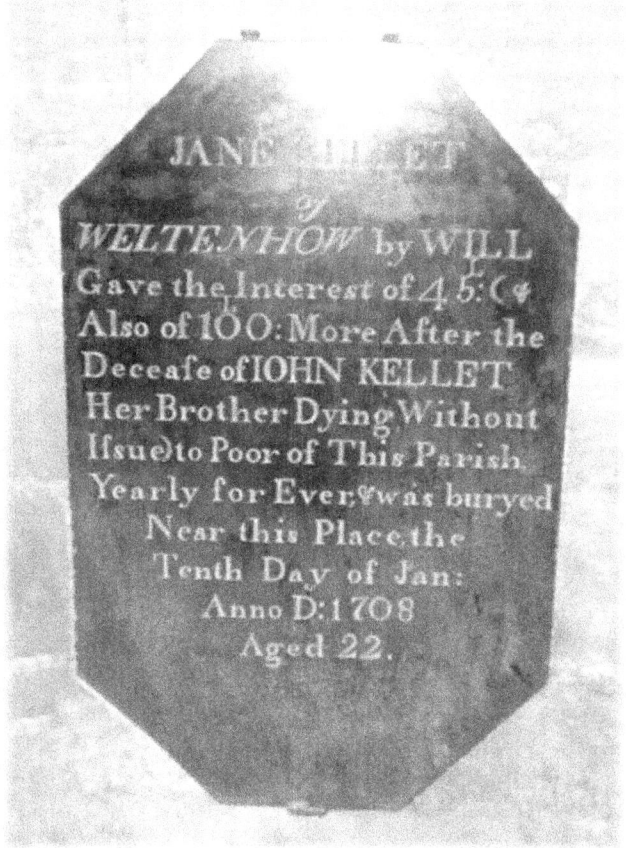

Authors Comment:
This stone is to be found in the interior wall of the Priory.
It appears, as far as I can make out, a total of £145 was to be given every year for ever to the poor of the parish. It was made up of an original £45 then when Iohn died without issue, a further £100 was added to the annual bequest. This would have been quite a gift for the period.

WILLIAM MAKEPEACE THACKERAY

Grave Text:
'William Makepeace Thackeray born July 18th 1811 died December 21st 1863.
Anne Carmichael Smyth died December 18th 1864 aged 72 his mother by her first marriage.'

Situated:
Kensal Green Cemetery, Harrow Road, London, W10 4RA, England.

Authors Comment:
This is a York Stone slab surrounded by railings. It looks rather grubby now but the engravings are still clear.

William Thackeray was a writer and editor who was born in Calcutta, India. His father was secretary to the board of the British East India Company. Thackeray was ranked second to Dickens in Victorian times and wrote such works as, "Vanity Fair" and "History of Henry Esmond". He died in 1863 and is said to have more or less ate and drank himself to death after his wife became insane and died.

ISAMBARD KINGDOM BRUNEL

Grave Text:
'Sir Marc Isambard Brunel Civil Engineer born at Macqueville in Normandy April 25th 1769 died in London December 12th 1845.
He has raised his own monument by his public works at Portsmouth, Chatham and The Thames Tunnel.
Dame Sophia Brunel widow of Sir Marc Isambard Brunel born February 18th 1775: died January 5th 1855.
Isambard Kingdom Brunel, Civil Engineer, only son of Sir Marc Isambard Brunel, born April 9th 1806: died September 15th 1859.
Mary Elizabeth Brunel, widow if Isambard Kingdom Brunel, born December 18th 1813: died August 25th 1881. Isambard Brunel D. C. L. Barrister-at-Law, son of Isambard Kingdom Brunel, Civil Engineer, born May 21 1837: died March 21

1903. Henry Marc Brunel, Civil Engineer, youngest son of Isambard Kingdom Brunel, Civil Engineer, Born June 27 1842: died October 7 1903.
Georgina Geils Donald widow of Isambard Brunel D. C. L. born October 30. 1836: died May 17. 1911. Lilian Sarah James, niece of Isambard Brunel D. C. L. born Nov 28. 1875: died Feb 17. 1929.'

Situated:
Kensal Green Cemetery, Harrow Road, London, W10 4RA, England.

Authors Comment:
Lovely block of white marble within the grave area marked out with a low row of cut stone with chamfered edges. Isambard Kingdom Brunel was one of Britain's greatest men. He was an Engineer and is best known for the creation of the Great Western Railway and a series of famous ocean-going steamships notably, 'The Great Eastern' and 'The Great Britain'. He built twenty five railways in all and one hundred and twenty five railway bridges, together with eight seaside piers and five suspension bridges.

His 'firsts' include, the first tunnel under a navigable river and the first propeller-driven ocean-going iron ship, 'The Great Britain', which at the time was the largest ship ever built.

Brunel died of a stroke after suffering with kidney problems aged 53.

JAMES IKIN NUNNERLEY

Grave Text:
'In loving memory of James Ikin Nunnerley, late of Lancers and one of The Six Hundred. Died November 22nd 1905 aged 74 years. "Nobly they fought and well".'

Situated:
Ormskirk Parish Church, St. Peter & St. Paul, Ormskirk, Lancashire, England.

Authors Comment:
Stone headstone rather weathered but still readable. It is found in Ormskirk Parish Church Churchyard, parts of which date back to 1170. Near the top is a skull and crossbones with "OR GLORY" under it and this is the Regimental Crest of the 17th Lancers, the skull being 'DEATH' hence 'Death or Glory'. The Regiment is famous for their part in the 'Charge of the Light Brigade' whilst fighting at the Battle of Balaclava in the Crimean War on Wednesday 25th October 1854.

Alfred, Lord Tennyson wrote a famous poem about the 'Charge' which starts as follows:

> "Half a league half a league,
> Half a league onward,
> All in the valley of Death
> Rode the six hundred:
> 'Forward, the Light Brigade!
> Charge for the guns' he said:
> Into the valley of Death
> Rode the six hundred."

Sergeant-Major Nunnerley was one of the six hundred who took part in the 'charge' and after the brief twenty minutes it took, was one of the 198 who were at the roll call after the event. His unusual middle name 'Ikin' was his mother's maiden-name.

After eleven years he left the army and held the position of Stationmaster at Disley for two years and then was appointed Drill Instructor to the Yeomanry Cavalry after receiving a request from Lord Skelmersdale. For his thirty three years in the army and yeomanry he received the princely sum of one shilling per day pension. After his service in the yeomanry he want back to his original occupation as he had been apprenticed to a draper. He opened a shop at 27 Moor Street in Ormskirk, his adopted town which is where he died.

W. H. DISRAELI OWEN

Grave Text:
'Erected in memory of W. H. Disraeli Owen of Hilbre-Island, who departed this life Sepr. 14th. 1869, Aged 6 months.
For of such is the kingdom of God. Mark.10 Ch. 14.V.'

Situated:
West Kirby Parish Church, St. Bridgets Church, West Kirby, Wirral, England.

Authors Comment:
A 'crisply' carved stone headstone which has not been weathered and stands proud although a little crooked due to sinking on one side. It has an ornate cross carved at the top, the ends of which are like Maple Tree leaves.
Hilbre Island is situated in the mouth of the estuary of the River Dee.
It is 47,000 square meters in size and is 1.6km from the coast of the mainland of the Wirral Peninsula. It is mentioned in the Doomsday Book as Chircheb West Kirkby with one church being on an island.
The island is tidal and can be reached on foot from the mainland at low tide and so is popular with tourists especially in the summer months.

.... MICHAELSON

Grave Text:
' ..... lyes ye body of .... Michaelson of ....enbanke who died this th.. day of May in .... year of his age, ...dom: 1723.'

Situated:
The Priory Church of St Mary & St Michael, Cartmel, Cumbria, England.

Authors Comment:
This gravestone is within the Priory and is an example of where a stone has apparently been cut to make a paving stone without a care for the person which the stone is there to commemorate. It is sad that this situation occurs but it is not the only example to be found, and not necessarily only in the Priory.

At the top is the skull and crossbones to signify 'death' and beneath is an hourglass, signifying 'the swift passing of time'. The hourglass is arranged on its side and looks like a bow-tie being worn by the skull.
It looks as if the 'e' from the word 'ye' was added as an afterthought as it is very small and above the writing course, however this may well have been the way it was written at the time.

K JONES

Grave Text:
'Er. cof. Am. K Jones. yr hon a fu farw tahc wedd 10 1837 oed 61.'

Situated:
Saint Deiniol Church, Llanddeiniolen, Arfon, Gwynedd, Wales.

Authors Comment:
Welsh slate headstone to K Jones. This is a plain stone and it is very crudely carved. One wonders if it was done by a family member perhaps as a mark of respect, or to reduce the funeral costs.

ANDREW DUCROW

Grave Text:
'The Family Tomb of Andrew Ducrow Erected Anno Domini 1837. Within this tomb erected by genius for the reception of its own remains are deposited those of Andrew Ducrow. Many years lessee of the Royal Amphitheatre, London , whose death deprived the arts and sciences of an eminent professor and liberal patron. His family of an affectionate husband and father, and the world of an upright man. He was born in London 10th Oct 1793, and died 27th Jan 1842, and to commemorate such virtues his afflicted widow has erected this tribute. Also of Andrew Ducrow ensign 40th Regiment, youngest son of the above. Who died of wounds received whilst gallantly leading his men in the attack on Rangariri, New Zealand, Nov 20th 1863. he was mentioned in despatches as being "if not the first certainly one of the first to enter the ………….. entrenchments". He died greatly beloved and deeply regretted by his brother officers and all who knew him. This tablet is erected to commemorate his noble death and as a small tribute of a great love by his sorrowing family. Peace to the memory of the brave. He was born 18th June …… and died   December …… .'

Situated:
Kensal Green Cemetery, Harrow Road, London, W10 4RA, England.

Authors Comment:
This is a vast Egyptian style monument designed by George Danson in 1837. Two sphinxes guard it. It is of plaster on brick with artificial stone moulded to shapes. There is a marble panel above the door and it has a marble broken column. There is a hat with gloves near by and a large damaged plaque on the side. It is grade II listed. There are two angels, signifying the fact that an angel is a messenger between God and man, one either side of the main plaque and two draped flags crossed beneath it. There is a large urn on the very top. Andrew Ducrow (snr) was a circus performer and owner. He raised the English circus to its peak and was known as the" Colossus of Equestrians". He had great horsemanship and his horse 'John Lump' died a few days after him. Andrew Ducrow (jnr) died fighting at the battle of

Rangirii for the British Army in the New Zealand land wars. His regiment were trying to take the Maori fortifications whilst under the command of General Cameron who later admitted his disapproval of the war which he believed was being deliberately waged for the benefit of land-hungry settlers. He resigned in 1865.

BJARNI PORDARSON

Grave Text:
'Bjarni Pordarson Fra Reykjaholum, F 23 April 1837, D 25 Mai 1918.
Porey Kr O....sdottir F 24/1 1848, D 26/1 1934.'

Situated:
Holavallagardur Cemetery, Reykjavik, Iceland.

Authors Comment:
This memorial is quite unusual as it is in the form of a tree with its branches cleanly cut off. It is made of stone or concrete with a black marble plaque. The plaque has a cross near the top above the text.
It blends in well with the real trees in the cemetery of which there are many.

HARRY MURDEN

Grave Text:
'This memorial stone was erected in affectionate remembrance of Harry Murden. Also of Jane Murden. The beloved wife of Harry Murden who died March 23rd 1884, aged 25 years. Henry, son of the above, died March 21st 1884, aged 2 days. Harry Murden the above who was killed at Bickerstaffe Colliery on June 12th 1884, aged 23 years. "Blessed are those servants whom the Lord when he cometh shall find watching" St Luke XIIc 37v'.

Situated:
All Saints Church, Rainford, Lancashire, England.

Authors Comment:
A stone monument with a pinnacle on the top. This is a memorial to the whole family who died within three months. It appears that Jane may have died in childbirth of Henry as she died two days prior to him. Harry then was tragically killed at the colliery. Bickerstaffe Colliery was one of many Lancashire coal mines in the area. It opened prior to 1853 and was owned by Bromilow Foster & Co Ltd., and Foster Williams & Co. Ltd.
In 1896 there were over 200 underground miners working there with John Foster as the Manager. It closed on 24th October 1936.

JOSEPH AND MARY RICHARDSON

Grave Text:
'The burial place of Joseph & Mary Richardson. He departed this life July 4th 1848 aged 49 years. She departed this life May 27th 1873 aged 71 years.
Joseph their grandson departed this life September 26th 1856 aged 9 months. Robert son of Joseph and Mary Richardson died October 1st 1866 aged 35 years. Not to be opened again.'

Situated:
All Saints Church, Rainford, Lancashire, England.

Authors Comment:
A grey marble tomb with engraving on both of the long sides. It is encircled by a chain metal ringed fence with metal posts and has two urns within the fence.

There is a most unexpected engraving on one end which reads "Not to be opened again". I have not seen this before on a grave and wonder why they thought that this was necessary but I suppose that there was good reason for this.

ALBERT OLIVER BRADLEY

Grave Text:
'Buried near this spot, 840882 L.SJT A. O. Bradley, Royal Artillery 14th – 16th February 1942 aged 27. Until the day break and shadows flee.'

Situated:
Kranji War Cemetery, Singapore.

Authors Comment:
Kranji War Cemetery has 4,458 Commonwealth casualties of the Second World War buried or commemorated there. Within the cemetery stands a memorial to 24,000 other casualties who have no known grave. The land forces commemorated by the memorial died during the campaigns in Malaya and Indonesia or in subsequent captivity, many of them during the construction of the Burma to Thailand railway, or at sea whilst being transported into imprisonment elsewhere.

Lance Sergeant Bradley was in the Royal Artillery and the regimental badge is on the headstone. The motto of the Royal Artillery shown also on the headstone is "Quo Fas Et Gloria Ducunt" which means "Whither Right And Glory Lead".

HONORE CHAMPION

Grave Text:
'Honore Champion, Edouard Champion 10 Octobre 1882 + 28 Fevrier 1938, Pierre Champion 28 Fevrier 1880 + 29 Juin 1942.'

Situated:
Le Cimetiere Montparnasse, Paris, France.

Authors Comment:
This is a fantastic tomb in white stone which was sculpted by Albert Bartholome. It shows Honore (1846 – 1913) in his library reading a book and it looks so lifelike. Honore was of course a librarian and an editor of books.
The father of historian Pierre

Champion, he founded "Editions Honore Champion" in 1874 and published scientific works for the layman in subjects such as history and literature.

JAMES DOBBS

Grave Text:
'In Memory of James Dobbs, Late Coachman at Scarisbrick Hall, Who died February 14 1879 Aged 51 years. Erected by the Count De Casteja'

Situated:
St Mark's Church, Scarisbrick, Merseyside, England.

Authors Comment:
Nice stone headstone with leaves carved near the top. The leaves meaning; regeneration, immortality and friendship. James was the Count's coachman at Scarisbrick Hall and he must have thought a lot of his servants to pay for the burial and grave. Next to this grave is that of William Ion, late policeman of Scarisbrick Hall which was also paid for by the Count. Scarisbrick Hall is a country house in Lancashire. It was the ancestral home of the Scarisbrick family and dates back to the 1100's. The present building was completed in 1867 and the architect was Augustus Pugin. It has a one hundred foot tower which strongly resembles the clock-tower of the Houses of Parliament in London.
The De Casteja family owned the hall from 1872 to 1923 when it was sold back to the Scarisbrick family. It is presently the home of Kingswood College a co-educational private day school. The building is Grade 1 listed and is on the Buildings At Risk Register.

FREDERIC BARTHOLDI

Grave Text:
'Sepulture Auguste F Bartholdi. Auteur Du Lion De Belfort Et De La Statue De La Liberte Eclairant Le Monde'.

Situated:
Le Cimetiere Montparnasse, Paris, France.

Authors Comment:
A fine grave, stone base with a tall red granite pillar on a red granite plinth. It has a large metal, probably bronze, angel with her right hand pointing straight up in the air towards heaven. On the granite pillar is a bronze portrait of Bartholdi and at the bottom is lain a drape, also in bronze. Known also as Amilcar Hasenfratz, Frederic Bartholdi (2nd August 1834 – 4th October 1904) was a sculptor. He is best known for his works of the Lion of Belfort and more especially The Statue of Liberty which is to be found in New York Harbour in the United States of America. The latter was donated to the USA in 1886 and its face is rumoured to be modelled on Bartholdi's mother, and the body that of his mistress. He was awarded a design patent in 1879 for the Statue of Liberty which also covered the sale of small copies of the statue which helped to raise the money to create the full statue. On the grave the angel is the messenger between God and man and the drape signifies mourning and mortality.

JOSEPH WORTHINGTON

Grave Text:
'In Loving memory of, Thy Will Be Done, Sapper Joseph Worthington R. E. The beloved son of Henry & Martha Worthington who was killed at Loos in France May 11th 1916, in his 21st year, interred Loos Cemetery France. Also Rhoda their beloved daughter who died Jany 22nd 1920 aged 22 months. Also Henry the above who died Nov 26th 1930 aged 55 years. Also Martha the above, who died June 10th 1948, aged 73 years. also Maurice son of the above, who died July 15th 1953, aged 48 years.
"Until The Day Dawn".

Situated:
All Saints Church, Rainford, Merseyside, England.

Authors Comment:
Stone headstone with a border of leaves and also a cluster of leaves at the top. Joseph was a Sapper, the definition of which is: one who digs saps; a soldier of the Royal Engineers; an official term for private. He is buried in the St. Patrick's Cemetery in Loos, France. The French cemetery gets its name from the fact that it was used largely by units of the 16th Irish Division in 1916. It has 595 burials of which 40 are unidentified and the graves of 23 which were destroyed by shell fire are now represented by special memorials. Its area is 3,001 square meters.

ROBERT THIBIER

Grave Text:
'Robert Thibier 1926 – 2001'.

Situated:
Le Cimetiere Montparnasse, Paris, France.

Authors Comment:
An extraordinary tomb which consists of a pair of large bronzed hands, about two meters high, holding a metal cross between its fingers. On the stone plinth is the name and dates on metal strips.
Robert Thibier was a Parisian designer and decorator.

JAMES LATHAM

Grave Text:
'……….. the rest In the soul of James Latham who died 7th June 1907 aged 79 years. "Eternal rest give to him o Lord, and let perpetual light shine upon Him". May he rest in peace Amen. Also Jane wife of the above died 25th March 1914 aged 85 years. Also Henry son of the above died 11th March 1919 aged 64 years. Also James Latham M.M. accidentally killed October 21st 1919 aged 24 years'.

Situated:
Saint Mary's Catholic Church, Little Crosby, Merseyside, England .

Authors Comment:
Stone gravestone which has IHS at the top which stands for In His Service. There are also ivy leaves either side of IHS meaning; Immortality, friendship and faithfulness. James Latham was unfortunate in that he was accidentally killed in 1919 after the 1st World War had finished. He had been awarded the M.M. which is the Military Medal.

This medal was awarded for bravery in battle on land and was awarded to ranks below commissioned rank, (the Military Cross being issued to higher ranks at the time). The medal was established on 25th March 1916 and was discontinued in 1993 as the Military Cross was then issued to all ranks. It is 36 mm diameter in silver. The reverse is inscribed "For Bravery In The Field". It has a dark blue ribbon 1.25 inches wide with five equal stripes of white, red, white, red and white.

HENRI RENE ALBERT GUY DE MAUPASSANT

Grave Text:
'GUY DE MAUPASSANT. Chacun garde au fond du coeur un souvenir qui ne veut pas mourir. Ces't un bruit de pas, le son d'une voix, un prenom ou un sourire. Chacun garde au fond du coeur une etoile de bonheur'.

Situated:
Le Cimetiere Montparnasse, Paris, France.

Authors Comment:
Quite a formal tomb made from white stone. It has double pillars holding a stone strip containing his name and above this a cross. Lower down is a wreath like shelf and on a lectern is an open book made from ceramics on which is the writing. The book is adorned by blue flowers and green leaves. The tomb is surrounded by short metal railings. Guy de Maupassant (5th August 1850 – 6th July 1893) was a French writer and is known as one of the fathers of the modern short story.

He was a contributing editor of several leading newspapers; Le Figaro, Gil Blas, Le Gaulois and L'Echo de Paris. His first masterpiece was entitled "Boule de Suif", published in 1880.

JOHN KEVIN MAGUIRE

Grave Text:
'………also Lieut. John Kevin Maguire, Irish Guards Killed in action in Normandy 4th Aug. 1944 Aged 21 years'.

Situated:
Saint Mary's Catholic Church, Little Crosby, Merseyside, England.

Authors Comment:
A clean cut granite ledger with a raised cross on top and on this in large letters R.I.P. Lieutenant Maguire is buried in the St. Charles de Percy War Cemetery in France which is found 44 kilometres south-west of Caen. He was in the 2nd Battalion Irish Guards, which landed in Normandy in June 1944 and took part in the advance from Seine to Nijmegen. The battle at Nijmegan was celebrated in the film "A Bridge Too Far" when the Allies tried to take a number of bridges over the Rhine including the bridges at Nijmegan and ultimately Arnhem.

CONSTANTIN BRANCUSI

Grave Text:
'Constantin Brancusi 1876 – 1957. Alexandre Istrati 1915 – 1991. Natalia Dumitresco 1915 – 1997. Demetra Istrati 1888 – 1975.'

Situated:
Le Cimetiere Montparnasse, Paris, France.

Authors Comment:
This grave is a simple one of white stone laid flat with the engraving on the top with a small cross above the writing. There is engraving also on one end, that of Demetra Istrati. It is surrounded by lovely plants and bright flowers. Brancusi was an internationally renowned Romanian sculptor. He was born in Hobita, Gorj near Targu Jiu, on 19th February 1876 and was a modernist sculptor. He worked in Auguste Rodin's studio but left after two months saying that "nothing can grow under big trees". Some of his works are: "The Kiss", "Sleeping Muse" and "The Endless Column", which is in Targu Jui, Romania. He died 16th March 1957.

THOMAS ORR

Grave Text:
'Consecrated to the memory of the undermentioned children of THOMAS and DEBORAH ORR of Cartmel, ANTHONY who died September 13TH 1814 AGED 11 ½ months. ANTHONY who died Novr. 3rd 1821 aged 3 weeks. RICHARD who died Decr.16th 1823 aged 15 months. Thomas who was unfortunately drowned near Peel July 4th 1824 aged 10 years and 9 months. THOMAS HUDSON who died Feby. 26th 1827, aged 2 years and 4 months. DEBORAH ORR their mother who died Novr. 1st 1842 aged 52 years. THOMAS ORR their father who died Augst. 14th 1843 aged 50 years'.

Situated:
The Priory Church of St Mary & St Michael, Cartmel, Cumbria, England.

Authors Comment:
A neat grey stone headstone showing the loss of five children from the Thomas and Deborah Orr family, plus their own deaths. Young Thomas was drowned near Peel aged 10 years and 9 months. Peel is one of three islands in Coniston Water, a lake in the English Lake District. It is said to be the original of the fictional Wild Cat Island which is portrayed in the book "Swallows and Amazons" which was written by Arthur Ransome. It is also the island near to where Donald Campbell was killed whilst trying to break the world water speed record in "Bluebird" in 1967.

JAMES (JIM) DOUGLAS MORRISON

Grave Text:
'James Douglas Morrison 1943 – 1971 Kata Ton Aimona Eaytoy.'

Situated:
Cimetiere du Pere Lachaise, Paris, France.

Authors Comment:
The grave is a rough granite block with a smooth granite surround. On the block is a brass name plate. The centre is filled with fresh flowers brought and left by his admirers. When I visited the grave, it was surrounded by barriers with a staff member keeping the hordes of fans in order. Jim Morrison was born on 8th December 1943 and was an American singer, poet, songwriter and film director. He is best known as the lead singer from the rock band "Doors". He was born in Melbourne, Florida, his father was an Admiral in the American Navy. He moved to Paris in 1971, which is where he made his last studio recording. Morrison died on 3rd July 1971 when he was found dead in a bathtub by Pamela Courson his long time companion. There was no autopsy on him as French law did not require one if the medical examiner found no evidence of foul play, which he had not.

EVAN NELSON

Grave Text:
'Evan Nelson, Four Breadths'.

Situated:
St Mary The Virgin, Rufford with Holmeswood, Rufford, Lancashire, England.

Authors Comment:
Stone gravestone neatly carved with very little on it except Evan's name and the words 'Four Breadths'. There are also two 'wheel like' carvings which may depict shining suns. Unfortunately there is no date of death or age. Possibly 18th century. The reference to breadths is probably designating the size of the burial plot so that no one disturbs the grave in the future. This could be because not all graves had a headstone and so it would, over time, be easy to dig a new grave and find a burial already there which had been forgotten. In the same cemetery there were other stones relating to four breadths and to two breadths.

SARAH BERNHARDT

Grave Text:
'Sarah Bernhardt 1844 – 1923.'

Situated:
Cimetiere du Pere Lachaise, Paris, France.

Authors Comment:
Quite a large tomb made from grey marble with open sides and ends and a marble coffin within. Gold writing displays the name and dates. Sarah Bernhardt was a French stage actress and was born in Paris 22nd October 1844, her parents were from Holland. She started her stage career in 1862 and was often referred to as "the most famous actress in history". She died on 26th March 1923 in the care of her son Maurice. Sarah Bernhardt has a star on the Hollywood Walk of Fame in America.

THOMAS HALLOWS

Grave Text:
'Sacred to the memory of Thomas Hallows late Quartermaster in the 3rd Regiment of Royal Lancashire Militia, and subsequently land agent for the Rufford Estates. Died July 7th 1858 aged 80 years'.

Situated:
St Mary The Virgin, Rufford with Holmeswood, Rufford, Lancashire, England.

Authors Comment:
Slightly subsiding headstone made from stone with carving still just as crisp as when it was created back in 1858, one hundred and fifty years ago. Thomas had a very responsible job in the Royal Lancashire Militia being the Quartermaster, looking after all the supplies. It is therefore reasonable that he would be offered such a responsible job as a land agent after leaving the Militia. The word Militia comes from the Latin

'Miles' meaning a soldier. They were a local defence force and in 1757 an act of Parliament was passed to create Militia to maintain order at home. This was because the main army was away fighting in the Seven Years War. The Lancashire Militia was originally formed in 1689. They eventually became part of the King's Regiment after numerous amalgamations.

EDITH PIAF

Grave Text:
'Famille Gasson – Piaf, Madame Lamboukas dite Edith Piaf 1915 – 1963, Theophanis Lamboukas dit Theo Sarapo 1936 – 1970, Louis Alphonse Gassion 1881 – 1944, Marcelle Dupont 1933 – 1935.'

Situated:
Cimetiere du Pere Lachaise, Paris, France.

Authors Comment:
A black marble tomb on a black marble plinth. It has a black marble cross with a metal statue of Christ being crucified on the cross. There is a black marble vase with the initials E P near the top of this cross. The cross is the emblem of faith. Edith Piaf born 19th December 1915 was a singer who is widely known as France's greatest pop singer. Her best known songs include; "Non, je ne regrette rien", "La vie en rose" and "Hymne a l'amour". She was born in Paris and was named Edith after Edith Cavell, who was a First World War nurse who helped French soldiers escape from German captivity, for which she was executed. Edith died of cancer on 10th October 1963 on the French Riviera. The grave is covered in flowers no doubt brought by her admirers.

DAVID BOOSIE

Grave Text:
'The burial place of David Boosie who died February 23rd 1853 aged 50 Years. Agent for the Rufford Estates from 1847 till the time of his Death'.

Situated:
St Mary The Virgin, Rufford with Holmeswood, Rufford, Lancashire, England.

Authors Comment:
A white marble headstone still clearly legible. David Boosie was Agent for the Rufford Estates for eight years until his early death aged fifty years. Rufford Old Hall's Estates would have required great management, and so agents would have been appointed to look after these. Rufford Old Hall was built in 1530 by Sir Thomas Hesketh. Only the Great Hall still stands now and it is in the hands of the National Trust. The Hall is said to be haunted by the Grey Lady who it is said is a young woman in a wedding dress awaiting the return of her betrothed, who was killed in battle. It is also said to be haunted by a man dressed in Elizabethan clothes and Elizabeth 1.

FREDERIC CHOPIN

Grave Text:
'A Fred Chopin. Frederic Chopin + Le 17th Octobre 1849. Frederic Chopin, ne en Pologne. A Zelazowa – Wola. Pres de Varsovie. Fils d'un Emigre Francais. Marie a Melle Krzyzanowska. Fille d'un Gentilhomme Polonais.'

Situated:
Cimetiere du Pere Lachaise, Paris, France.

Authors Comment:
A sparkling white marble female statue sitting with head bowed. This is on a white stone block which has the outline carved of Chopin's head. It is surrounded by black metal railings with white carved posts. The letters F C are within the front railings. Frederic Chopin was born 1st March 1810 in Poland. He was a great piano composer who amongst others wrote: "The Minute Waltz" and "Revolutionary". He moved to Paris in the 1830's where he died in 1849. This was the year after the French Revolution in 1848, which saw the end of the reign of King Louis Philippe. There is a Post-mortem cast of Chopin's left hand to be found in the Polish Museum at Rapperswil.

TOMBE OF THE FRENCH UNKNOWN SOLDIER

Grave Text:
'Ici Repose un Soldat Francais Mort Pour la Patrie 1914 – 1918.'

Situated:
The Arc de Triomphe, Paris, France.

Authors Comment:
This is a magnificent situation to locate the French Tomb of their Unknown Soldier from World War One. The body was placed here in 1920 and an eternal flame burns on the memorial. The inscription translates as; "Here Lies a French Soldier Who Died For His fatherland 1914 - 1918".

The Arc de Triomphe was commissioned by Napoleon I after his victory at Austerlitz in 1806. He wanted to take his new bride, Marie-Louise through the Arc on their wedding day, but as it was not complete, a temporary wooden one was constructed for this purpose. It was finally completed in 1836 when King Louis Philippe was on the throne.

OSCAR WILDE

Grave Text:
'Oscar Wilde, Author of Salome and other beautiful works, was born at 21 Westland Row, Dublin October 16 1854. He was educated at Portora Royal School, Enniskillen and Trinity College, Dublin, where he obtained a Scholarship and won the Berkeley Gold Medal for Greek in 1874. Sometime Demy of Magdalen College in Oxford he gained a first-class in Classic Moderations in 1876: a first-class in Literae Humanicres and the Newgate Prize for English Verse in 1878. He died fortified by the Sacraments of the Church at the Hotel D'Alsace, 13 Rue des Beauxarts, Paris. R.I.P. .... Job XX1X.22..........................'

Situated:
Cimetiere du Pere Lachaise, Paris, France.

Authors Comment:
This is a very large white stone monument to a great novelist, poet, playwright and writer of short stories. It has carved a winged man's body wearing a head-dress. The man's genitals have been removed, and the monument is

covered in graffiti and "lipstick kisses" from his admirers, despite these words which are found on a metal plaque on the base of the monument: "Respect the memory of Oscar Wilde and do not deface this tomb. It is protected by law as an Historic Monument and was restored in 1992". The tomb was designed by sculptor Sir Jacob Epstein. Oscar Fingal O'Flahertie Wills Wilde died from Meningitis on 30th November 1900.

ANDRE CITROEN

Grave Text:
'Famille Andre Citroen. Solange Citroen 21 Janvier 1924 – 22 Novembre 1925. Madame Andre Citroen nee Georgina Bingen 27 Avril 1892 – 20 Fevrier 1955. Madame Maxine Citroen nee Antoinette David-Weill Chevalier De L'Ordre du Merite 3 Septembre 1920 – 15 Octobre 1980, Madame Bernard Citroen nee Piroska Szabo 6 Octobre 1919 – 4 Decembre 1996, Andre Citroen Grand Officier De La Legion D'Honneur 5 Fevrier 1878 – 3 Juillet 1935, Maxime Citroen Officier De La Legion D'Honneur 27 Mai 1919 – 11 Mars 1990, Madame Jacqueline Citroen Chevalier De La legion D'Honneur 11 Septembre 1915 – 28 Mars 1994, Bernard Citroen Commandeur De La Legion D'Honneur 4 Juin 1917 – 9 Aout 2002.'

Situated:
Le Cimetiere Montparnasse, Paris, France.

Authors Comment:
An elegant Grey marble tomb with two full length planters, one either side of main tomb. Marble posts and chains

surround. Andre Gustave Citroen, born 5th February 1878, was the founder of Citoen Automobile company in 1919. He also invented double helical gears. Andre died in Paris 3rd July 1935 from cancer. He has the Parc Andre Citroen (a public park) named after him in Paris.

ALFRED DREYFUS

Grave Text:
'Lieutt. Colonel Alfred Dreyfus, Officier La Legion D'Honneur 9 Octobr 1859 – 12 Juillet 1935. A La Memoire De Madeleine Levy deportee Par Les Allemands Disparue a Aushwitz a l'age de 25 Ans. Mme Alfred Dreyfus nee Lucie Hadamard 23 Aout 1869 – 14 Decembre 1945. Pierre Dreyfus 5 Avril 1891 – 28 Decembre 1946. Mme Jeanne Levy nee Dreyfus 22 Fevrier 1893 – 30 Avril 1981. Mme Pierre Dreyfus nee Marie Baur 15 Juin 1900 – 29 Decembre 1987. Docteur Etienne

Levy Officier De La Legion D'Honneur 17 Fevrier 1922 – 2 Juillet 1996.'

Situated:
Le Cimetiere Montparnasse, Paris, France.

Authors Comment:
A simple stone grave with the stone laid flat. On the stone is all the writing and all around it has been placed small stones, presumably by visitors to the grave. There is Hebrew writing at the top of the stone which translated means "Here Lies". Alfred Dreyfus was an artillery officer who was tried and convicted of treason in 1894. The case was known world wide as the Dreyfus Affair. He was convicted of passing details of some new artillery to the Germans but in 1896 further evidence was found which led to his exoneration in 1906. The day after this he was readmitted into the French army as a Major. He died in 1935 aged 75.

MARY KELLY

Grave Text:
'Mary Kelly died March 5th 1837 aged 82 years, Fifty Seven Years a servant with William Field. John Sharp A Partner in Service with the above for Thirty Two Years died January the 10th 1839 aged 53.'

Situated:
The Priory Church of St Mary & St Michael, Cartmel, Cumbria, England.

Authors Comment:
A slate headstone in the outside wall of the Priory. Mary Kelly served for a grand total of fifty seven years for William Field which was probably her whole working life. Such dedication. In the June of the year that Mary died, Queen Victoria succeeded to the British throne and in the July of the same year she moved into Buckingham Palace to become the first monarch to reside there. The year prior to her partner in service, John Sharp dying, 16th November 1838 sees the Boers defeating the Zulu warriors at the Battle of Blood River in South Africa.

JULES DUMONT D'URVILLE

Grave Text:
'Monument Eleve Par Les Soins De La Societe de Geographie Navigation Geographie Histoire Naturelle Philologie. Ie Voyage dans les mers du levant. IIe Voyage au tour du monde. III Voyage autour du monde pole sud. Geographie botanique, Debris du nauf e de la laperouse rapports, Terre Louis Phillippe, Terre Adelie, Jules Sebastien Cesar Dumont D'Urville Mort le 8 Mai 1842 age de 51 ans. Adolphe Eugene Jules Dumont D'urville, Mort le 23 Janvier 1832 age de 21 mois. Adele

Dorothee Dumont D'Urville nee Perin, Mort le 8 Mai 1842 age de 48 ans. Jules Eugene Hector Dumont D'Urville, Mort le 8 Mai 1842 age de 16 ans.'

Situated:
Le Cimetiere Montparnasse, Paris, France.

Authors Comment:
This monument is in the form of an extremely large column and is covered in carvings in the white stone. I have only copied a small amount of what is carved on it. It is at least twenty feet high and is covered not just with words but boats and people. It describes the exploring that Jules D'Urville did in his life time. He visited New Zealand, Australia, The South and Western Pacific and Antarctica. Born 23rd May 1790 he was a Naval Officer and Explorer. His death was tragic as he and all his family were killed in the first ever French train crash on 8th May 1842 on there way to Versailles.

PIERRE PROVOST

Grave Text:
'Symbole de la Brigade Fabien Devenue le 151e R.I. Ici reposent a cote de leur chef. Celui qui croyait en dieu Le Sergent Pierre Provost F.F.I. tombe a Gravelotte (Moselle) le 26 Septembre 1944 a l'age 25 ans dans les rangs de la Brigade Fabien. Celui qui n'y croyait pas le 2e classe Albert Bodere F.T.P.F. tombe au passage du Rhin le 3 Avril 1945 a l'age du 13 ans ……..'

Situated:
Cimetiere du Pere Lachaise, Paris, France.

Authors Comment:
This monument is to two members from the Brigade Fabien. Colonel Fabien (Pierre Georges) was one of two members of the French Communist Party who carried out the first assassinations of German personnel during the Second World War in Occupied France. He joined the French Resistance in 1940 and was killed in 1944 by a landmine in Alsace. There is a Paris Metro station called Colonel Fabien and the Place du Colonel Fabien which are both named after him. The French Communist Party HQ is in Place du Colonel Fabien.

JAMES DE ROTHSCHILD

Grave Text:
'James Alain De Rothschild 1910 – 1982. Il sut aimer, tous ceux qui l'ont, connu ou simplement croise cherissent la memoire d'un home bon, d'une simplicite rayonnante, au Coeur resolu et grand ouvert aux problemes des homes, son engagement envers la communaute, sa fidelite a la torah granddissant avec lage et les epreuyes lui donnent au jugement de ses pairs une place parmi les justes. Aux hommes du l'avenir il laisses sa vie a mediter…….'.

Situated:
Cimetiere du Pere Lachaise, Paris, France.

Authors Comment:
This is a huge family vault in white stone with a R (and reverse R) motife on the front. It has a bright green door. All the memorials are inside and are difficult to read with the exception of the one above. The Rothschild banking empire was founded in 1812 in Paris by James Mayer Rothschild, who was a German from Frankfurt. His father sent James to Paris and his brothers all over Europe to establish the family business.

CHARLES PIGEON

Grave Text:
'Famille Charles Pigeon. Madame Charles Pigeon nee Leonie Martin 1846 – 1909. Charles Pigeon, Chevalier De La Legion d'Honneur 1838 – 1915.'

Situated:
Le Cimetiere Montparnasse, Paris, France.

Authors Comment:
This grave is the most unusual I have ever seen. It is in the form of a double bed with Mr and Mrs Pigeon in bed together. Mrs is lying down whilst Mr is reading a book propped on his right arm. It is adorned around by flower boxes and looks altogether a nice monument made from marble with a cross on the top of the headboard. There is an angel statue with her hand raised aloft on the very top. The angel is the messenger between God and man.
Charles Pigeon was the inventor of a non exploding gas lamp. It was patented in 1884 and was presented at the Universal Exhibition of 1900.
He died in Paris on the 18th March 1915.

INDEX OF ENTRIES

Aikman, Col Frederick Robertson (V. C.)	107
Alexander, William	39
Allen, Mary	20
Anderson, John	68
Atkinson, Jane	117
Babbage, Charles	105
Bartholdi, Frederic	136
Bernhardt, Sarah	149
Blake, William	64
Blanchard, James	34
Bligh, William	84
Blondin, Charles (Gravelet-Blondin)	99
Bonnar, John	78
Boosie, David	153
Bradley, Albert Oliver	133
Brancusi, Constantin	145
Breidfjord, Sigurdur	101
Browne, Beatrice Blore	56
Brunel, Isambard Kingdom	121
Buckland, John (and Worth, Thomas)	15
Bunyan, John	63
Carroll, John	48
Champion, Honore	134
Chopin, Frederic	154
Citroen, Andre	160
Concanon, Christopher	65
De-Foe, Daniel	61
De Rothschild, James	169
Dickens, Cedric Charles	89
Disraeli Owen, W. H.	125
Dobbs, James	135
Doulton, Sir Henry	79
Dreyfus, Alfred	162
Ducrow, Andrew	128
D'Urville, Jules Dumont	165
Edwards, Catherine	93
Einarsson, Sigfus	106
Foster, John	24

Gauntlett, Dr Henry John	92
Graham, Frank Christopher	12
Gravelet-Blondin, Jean Francois (Charles)	99
Guomundsson, Erlendur	109
Guy de Maupassant, Henri R A	142
Hafstein, Hannes	116
Hallows, Thomas	150
Hornby, Frank	59
Hughes, Richard	17
Husbands, Harriet	13
Jones, Catherine	91
Jones E (Slack, Edwin)	28
Jones, Henry (and Jones, John)	96
Jones, John (and Jones, Henry)	96
Jones, K	127
Jones, Capt Thomas S	32
Kellet, Jane	119
Kelly, Mary	164
Latham, James	140
Liverpool Orphan Boys' Asylum	22
Lloyd, Pierce	16
Locke, Joseph	102
Lort, William F.R.G.S.	35
McDonald, Frank W (and McDonald, J.M)	81
McDonald, J. M (and McDonald, Frank W)	81
McGarvie, E	88
McGrigor, James	73
Magnusdottir, Gudridur	118
Maguire, John Kevin	144
Maxim, Sir Hiram S	67
Michaelson, ……..	126
Milne, Peter	41
Morrison, James (Jim) Douglas	147
Muggur (Thorsteinsson, Gudmundur)	98
Murden, Harry	131
Murray, John C (Jack)	46
Nelson, Evan	148
Nicoll, John (and Wilson, Helen)	70
Noonan, Robert	54
Nunnerley, James Ikin	123

Ollivierre, Ormand J	27
Orr, Thomas	146
Owen, W. H. Disraeli	125
Paisson, Pordur	104
Penny, Capt William	74
Piaf, Edith	151
Pigeon, Charles	171
Pordarson, Bjarni	130
Potts, William	110
Price, Arthur	66
Provost, Pierre	167
Rawling, Jonathan	57
Reith, George	44
Remains of an Unknown Australian Soldier	77
Richardson, Sergeant A. H. L. (V. C.)	18
Richardson, Joseph (and Richardson, Mary)	132
Richardson, Mary (and Richardson, Joseph)	132
Riddell, John Scott	83
Sigurdsson, Gudjon	111
Simpson, Thomas	112
Skinner, James Scott	86
Slack, Edwin (Jones E)	28
Smith, George (and Smith, Kitty)	38
Smith, Kitty (and Smith, George)	38
Smith, William Henry	94
Soldier of the Great War	14
Spurgeon, Charles Haddon	71
Stokes, Lena	11
Tate, Sir Henry	76
Thackeray, William Makepeace	120
Thibier, Robert	139
Thorsteinsson, Gudmundur (Muggur)	98
Trollope, Anthony	90
Turner, Sir Llewelyn	36
Unknown Soldier, Tomb of the French	156
Verne, Jules	9
Watt, Alexander Aitken	42
Webber, Henry	52
Wilde, Henry T	25
Wilde, Oscar	158

Williams, Capt Hugh	30
Wilson, Helen (and Nicoll, John)	70
Winn, Peter	50
Wordsworth, William	114
Worth, Thomas (and Buckland, John)	15
Worthington, Joseph	138
Wyard, Emma	58

www.ingramcontent.com/pod-product-compliance
Lightning Source LLC
Chambersburg PA
CBHW072135160426
43197CB00012B/2115